The Epistemology of
A Priori Knowledge

THE EPISTEMOLOGY OF
A PRIORI KNOWLEDGE

Tamara Horowitz

Edited by
Joseph L. Camp, Jr.

UNIVERSITY PRESS

2006

OXFORD
UNIVERSITY PRESS

Oxford University Press, Inc., publishes works that further
Oxford University's objective of excellence
in research, scholarship, and education.

Oxford   New York
Auckland   Cape Town   Dar es Salaam   Hong Kong   Karachi
Kuala Lumpur   Madrid   Melbourne   Mexico City   Nairobi
New Delhi   Shanghai   Taipei   Toronto

With offices in
Argentina   Austria   Brazil   Chile   Czech Republic   France   Greece
Guatemala   Hungary   Italy   Japan   Poland   Portugal   Singapore
South Korea   Switzerland   Thailand   Turkey   Ukraine   Vietnam

Copyright © 2006 by Oxford University Press, Inc.

Published by Oxford University Press, Inc.
198 Madison Avenue, New York, New York 10016

www.oup.com

Oxford is a registered trademark of Oxford University Press

Library of Congress Cataloging-in-Publication Data
Horowitz, Tamara.
The epistemology of a priori knowledge / Tamara Horowitz ;
edited by Joseph L. Camp, Jr.
p.   cm.
Includes bibliographical references and index.
ISBN-13 978-0-19-518271-2
ISBN 0-19-518271-5
1. A priori. I. Camp, Joseph L., Jr. II. Title.
BD181.3.H67 2005
121'.3—dc22   2004063611

1 3 5 7 9 8 6 4 2

Printed in the United States of America
on acid-free paper

*Tamara would have dedicated this book
to her father, mother, and brother, not only
because she loved them, but because she
learned from their example that creativity
must be combined with hard work.*

Joseph L. Camp, Jr.

ACKNOWLEDGMENTS

Tamara discussed the arguments in these essays with many colleagues, friends, and students. I know that she made changes in the way she approached the themes of her "Backtracking Fallacy" argument as a result of discussions with David Gauthier, Anil Gupta, Mark Wilson, and Wes Salmon. I am sure there were others who should be mentioned.

Anil Gupta and Jeremy Heis read my edited versions of the unpublished essays at different stages of completion and helped me get things as nearly right as I could. Connie Hrabovsky and Collie Henderson saw to the final manuscript preparation. I am greatly indebted to them all.

I am grateful to the *Journal of Philosophy* for kind permission to reprint "A Priori Truth," originally published in the *Journal of Philosophy* 82, 5 (1985): 225–239; to the Center for the Philosophy of Science at the University of Pittsburgh for kind permission to reprint "Newcomb's Problem as a Thought Experiment," originally published in *Thought Experiments in Science and Philosophy*, ed. Tamara Horowitz and Gerald J. Massey (Savage, Md.: Rowman and Littlefield, 1991), 305–316; to the University of Chicago Press for kind permission to reprint "Philosophical Intuitions and Psychological Theory," originally published in *Ethics* 108 (1998): 367–385; and to Kluwer Academic Publishers for kind permission to reprint "Stipulation and Epistemological Privilege," originally published in *Philosophical Studies* 44 (1983): 305–318.

CONTENTS

The Epistemology of
A Priori Knowledge

INTRODUCTION

Joseph L. Camp, Jr.

W hen Tamara Horowitz died early in 2000, she was Chair of the Department of Philosophy at the University of Pitts-burgh (the first woman to chair the department). She had published several articles, most of them on the epistemology of a priori knowledge and a priori methods of reasoning. The four previously published essays in this collection are concerned with these topics, as are the two previously unpublished essays.

Tamara also left a very large quantity of writing, in stages of completion ranging from notes to drafts of articles and book chapters. The greater part of this material also concerned the epistemology of the a priori, though a substantial part was concerned with problems of feminist philosophy.

In the years just before she became ill with the brain cancer that rapidly took her life, Tamara was hard at work on a book. Eventually the focus of this book project came to be the "sure-thing" argument in decision theory. After her death, I assembled, edited, and substantially rewrote much of the material she had produced for inclusion in her planned book, as she had requested me to do. The result is "The Backtracking Fallacy," a monograph-length essay included in this collection.

Tamara had not settled on final formulations of many of the arguments and definitions in this work. Usually there were several, sometimes conflicting, drafts. And none of the drafts were written in polished, final-draft style. Some arguments she spent months working on she eventually decided did not belong in her book at all. Fortunately, she and I had discussed all the parts of her book project many times, so I had some idea how she might have chosen to develop arguments that were left unfinished. Nevertheless, I was not always sure how she would have written various parts of the book, and substituted my own judgment when that seemed necessary, staying as close as I could to the points I believed she wanted to make, and the order in which I believed she wanted to make them. As a result, there doubtless are flaws in argument and in formulation that must be attributed entirely to me, not to Tamara.

I am deeply grateful to Anil Gupta for carefully reading an earlier draft of "The Backtracking Fallacy," for correcting a number of errors I had made, and suggesting many other improvements.

I assembled a short essay, "Making Rational Choices When Preferences Cycle," from draft material Tamara planned to combine into a single article. All of these drafts were much more polished, and mutually consistent, than the material that became "The Backtracking Fallacy." All I had to do was write some initial background material, and fit her drafts together as seamlessly as I could.

None of Tamara's writing on feminist philosophy is in this collection. I hope (and believe) that others, who are competent to edit this material for publication, will do so in the near future.

I wish I could read and reread the book on sure-thing reasoning Tamara would have completed herself, had she lived in good health for one more year.

Let me turn now to some comments on the essays in this collection. Tamara often described herself as a "naturalist" as a philosopher. That suggests that her preferred philosophical method was to construct philosophical arguments on the basis of scientific results, or to use scientific results to rebut philosophical arguments. Sometimes her philosophy was naturalistic in that sense, but often it was not. Her naturalism was broadly humanistic. She believed that far too many philosophers, especially those in the analytic tradition, with which she was most familiar, prize universality in their theories to such a degree that they are willing to abstract from many widely shared and philosophically important human traits, because taking account of these traits would force them to accept limitations on the scope of their theories. If we take these human traits seriously, we may need to make do with less sweeping and less "elegant" theories, but we will learn much that is of lasting philosophical value.

Although Tamara's philosophical work was divided between the epistemology of the a priori and feminist philosophy, I will discuss only the way her humanistic naturalism expressed itself in her epistemology, since all the essays in this collection are epistemological. Tamara was convinced that traditional epistemologists of the a priori make two closely related mistakes: They set the standard for a priority too high, dismissing—as irrelevant errors of evaluation or cognition—features of reasoning that ought, instead, be seen as important aspects of a priori inference. And they are inclined to classify as fallacies certain aspects of a priori inference that ought, instead, be classified as rationally permissible though not rationally mandatory. These philosophers ignore, as the clutter one would expect to find in the reasoning of untrained thinkers, much that should be integral to our understanding of the a priori; much that makes the philosophical study of the a priori exciting and rewarding.

In her passionate attachment to this belief, Tamara reminded me of the later Wittgenstein (an analogy she did not like at all) and of Bishop Berkeley (an analogy she liked even less). She did not remind me of Carnap, perhaps her philosophical idol, in this respect, though in another respect, a belief in the unqualified importance of *precision* in philosophical thought, she was very like Carnap.

Let me say something about how Tamara's humanistic naturalism drives the argument of each of the essays in this collection. Since I must be brief, and let her ideas stand on their own—as it will be obvious to the reader they do—I must leave out mention of a great deal that she thought, rightly, was valuable in these essays.

I'll begin with "A Priori Truth." She argues, carefully, for an explication in "traditional" fashion of the concept of an a priori truth, and then recommends a reinterpretation of that explication. Skipping some subtleties that she includes, her explication proceeds through the following stages.

> a can know p independently of experience if and only if in every world in which a exists, p is true, and a has the concepts in p, a has enough experience to know p.[1]

> "This definition does not imply that a actually knows p in the worlds that meet the conditions set forth in the antecedent, but implies only that in such a world a has all the experience necessary *to come to know p* simply by ratiocination."[2]

Finally,

> A truth p is a priori if and only if everyone can know p independently of experience.[3]

The problem arises when we consider the generally accepted a priority of mathematics. I will let Tamara's own words tell the story:

> Nearly all mathematical knowledge requires accepting, as reasons for accepting some theory, propositions analogous to "I proved lemma L earlier" or "I remember that lemma L has been established."
>
> Some philosophers of mathematics—Frege, for instance—have written as though the epistemology of mathematics, unlike the epistemology of everything else, should make reference only to mathematical propositions and not to such propositions as "I constructed a good proof of L_9 from two lemmas I proved last week." A mathematician's evidence for accepting a theorem is idealized as isomorphic to a formal proof—a sequence of "steps," each a *mathematical* proposition....
>
> Imagine an epistemologist of perception saying that my evidence for "This is a tomato" may include "This is red" but *not* "I have not forgotten how red things look under these conditions." In fact the body of accepted propositions a mathematician must know to be true (and that must not be overridden) in order to be justified in accepting a theorem nearly always includes *much* more than "purely mathematical" propositions.[4]

After some reflection on this anomaly of the epistemology of mathematics, Tamara draws her conclusion:

> I suggest a compromise. We should reject the incorrigibility of mathematical knowledge. We should philosophically explain the certainty of mathematical knowledge as due to a very great difference between the properties of mathematical errors, and, for example, those of errors in the empirical sciences. Finally, we should construe 'ratiocination' in my explanation of the a priori broadly enough to count mathematical truths as a priori in the event they are provable, and treat mathematical truth as the *defining stereotype* for a priori truth. Let me explain:
>
> Consider a mathematician who is proceeding through a proof. He has proved lines L_7 and L_8 and he says (or thinks) line L_9, which follows validly from L_7 and L_8. But he does not remember whether he proved L_7 or simply assumed it as a hypothesis. Observers he has every reason to trust tell him he did not prove L_7. Clearly he has insufficient

evidence to justify his accepting L_9, though he has proved it. Of course this example assumes an especially feeble memory, but no human can hold all of a very complicated mathematical theory in mind. One must trust memories, one must trust that symbols in a notebook have not been changed so as to mislead, and one must trust textbooks and colleagues at least as supports for one's own apparent memories. In general the evidence possessed by a mathematician for a theorem can be overridden by any of a great variety of further evidential inputs. . . .

Is it not odd, then, that mathematics has been accorded privileged status as an a priori science?

It is not odd. The "empirical" mistakes a mathematician can make are (or were before machine theorem-proving entered the picture) different from the mistakes open to other scientists in two important ways. They are *technologically simple* to look for, and they are plausibly supposed to be *unsystematic*. A clerical error, misprint, or faulty memory can be discovered by easy checking procedures available at all times to a mathematician and to his research community. . . . Where I slip up, you will not. . . . If mathematics were done in isolation or if there were *many* cases of trick proofs that tend to seduce everyone alike, *our attitudes would be very different.* Natural scientists are not so well off. Everybody who watches the amoebas divide in microscope illumination may see them divide in two when in fact they divide in three in the dark. Delicate indirect testing is needed to show that *all* biologists are not systematically misled in such ways. . . .

These differences between mathematics and natural science are the foundation of our intuition that mathematical knowledge is especially *certain*, and completely justify preferential treatment for mathematics. It *should* be called an a priori science. And it should be the *stereotypical* system of a priori knowledge. The way to get that effect, given my explication of the a priori, is to treat looking something up in a different book, or noticing that you tend to make algebraic mistakes when you are hungry though not otherwise, as part of "ratiocination." . . . My suggestion is that such experiences should be counted as elements in ratiocinative thought when (a) we must so count them in order to make everything evidentially relevant to a given piece of mathematical knowledge turn out to be pure ratiocination, or (b) when they occur in some sequence of experiences that, though it does not lead to mathematical knowledge, is intuitively *very like* some experience-sequence that would lead to mathematical knowledge, and that does lead to the having of some piece of knowledge about something, and in which the experience in question must be included so as to include everything evidentially relevant to the piece of knowledge in question. That is, what is a priori should be adjusted to fit what is done in actual mathematical practice. In the correct epistemological order, it should not be a *discovery* that the truths of mathematics are a priori. What should be a discovery is that some truths of other subject matters are a priori, that is, "mathlike."[5]

I have quoted at length from Tamara's concluding argument in "A Priori Truth" to show how a humanistic position in epistemology can be developed and defended. One starts with the fact that in order to have some bit of mathematical knowledge, the mathematician's evidence must include much that is not directly mathematical. No clerical errors have inadvertently changed the meaning of lines of proof written down a few days ago and not remembered perfectly, no inference in the argument just keeps looking valid to *this* mathematician, due to some idiosyncrasy, when it would not look valid to any other mathematician. There are two ways to go with facts like these: One way is to say that the thinking and inquiring one does in order to learn that such errors have not occurred is incidental to the practice of mathematics, it is not part of *mathematical* ratiocination. The other way is to say that this "error-eliminating" thought *is* part of specifically mathematical practice.

Tamara sees the epistemological tradition as having opted for the first way. She opts for the second, thereby letting mundane human glitches, and efforts to correct them, qualify as part of math. Tamara's way has a considerable virtue: We are led to think seriously about these glitches, about how the glitches a mathematician needs to worry about differ from the errors a natural scientist needs to worry about.

What we discover are interesting and important differences. These differences are well enough defined that Tamara can suggest that when the "mathlike" pattern of glitches is all one has to worry about, it makes sense to say the truths one is learning are "a priori." The traditional approach would never have led to this insight, because the very human glitch-proneness of mathematicians would be dismissed from the start as epistemologically irrelevant.

"A Priori Truth" is a medium-length article that argues for a large philosophical conclusion: how the concept of an a priori truth should be understood. "The Backtracking Fallacy" is a monograph-length essay discussing a single, allegedly a priori, pattern of reasoning. The easiest way to get a sense for Tamara's philosophical aims in "The Backtracking Fallacy" is to think about her reasons for structuring most of it as a dialog between two friends, "Jack" and "Casey," who enjoy discussing philosophy.

But first, a quick summary of the pattern of inference that is Tamara's topic (and the topic of the conversations between "Jack" and "Casey").

In his classic book on the theory of rational choice *The Foundations of Statistics*, Leonard Savage recommended a principle of inference he called the "sure-thing principle," saying that it had nearly the status of a law of logic. As a sample of inference following the sure-thing principle, Savage asked his readers to imagine a businessman who is trying to decide whether to buy a certain piece of property:

> A businessman contemplates buying a certain piece of property. He considers the outcome of the next presidential election relevant to the attractiveness of the purchase. So, to clarify the matter for himself, he asks whether he would buy if he knew that the Republican candidate were going to win, and he decides that he would do so. Similarly he considers whether he would buy if he knew that the Democratic candidate were going to win, and again finds that he would do so. Seeing that he would buy in either event, he decides that he should buy, even though he does not know which event obtains, or will obtain, as we would ordinarily say.[6]

Savage formulates the sure-thing principle in several ways. Tamara uses a formulation that almost, but not quite, parallels one of Savage's formulations (the difference is a simplification that does not affect her argument):

Principle B (for "backtracking"):

Suppose an agent is trying to decide beween two possible actions, f and g. Let e_1 be the state of knowledge of this agent at the time she is making her decision. Suppose the agent knows she will receive information that will put her in one or the other of two possible states of knowledge, e_2 or e_3. Assume that e_2 and e_3 exclude each other, and exhaust the possible states of knowledge the agent may be in upon receiving further information—or rather, they exhaust the possible states of knowledge she may be in that would be relevant to her choosing between performing f and performing g.

> Clause (1): Assume that if the agent were to be in e_2, she would see that she *should not have chosen f* over g; and moreover, if she were to be in e_3 she would see that she *should have chosen g* over f. And assume she can see that these things are so even when she is still in e_1. Then, *even when she is still in e_1*, she should choose to perform g rather than f.
> Clause (2): Assume that if the agent were to be in either e_2 or e_3, she would see that she *should have chosen g* over f, and assume that she can see that these things are so even when she is still in e_1. Then, even when she is still in e_1, she should choose to perform g rather than f.[7]

Clause (1) of Principle B is similar to what is often called "the weak dominance principle," and clause (2) is similar to what is often called "the strong dominance principle." The difference is that the alternative possibilities e_1, e_2, and e_3 mentioned in each clause of Principle B are alternative states of knowledge the decision-maker might be in, whereas the alternative possibilities appealed to in the dominance principles are logical or metaphysical possibilities. (Tamara was not sure that people who use the dominance principles always make a clear distinction between "epistemic" possibilities and logical or metaphysical possibilities).

The Businessman Argument follows clause (2) of Principle B. Some other arguments discussed in "The Backtracking Fallacy" follow clause (1) instead. Now, back to the role of the dialog structure.

Until the very end of the essay, "Casey" is a staunch defender of sure-thing reasoning. He has made a careful study of the topic. "Jack," on the other hand, knows next to nothing about such things at the start of their many friendly debates. As time goes by, Jack becomes more sophisticated, and eventually has very thoughtful replies to Casey's arguments. Casey is intellectually honest, and presents his untutored friend with decision problems he guesses Jack will answer in ways that violate the sure-thing principle. This is just what Jack does.

At the center of the debate between Casey and Jack are decision problems that elicit a "non-sure-thing" answer from a majority of people, as psychological experiments have shown. Moreover, people who give non-sure-thing answers tend to stick to their first, intuitive, answer even when it is explained to them that sure-thing reasoning dictates a different answer. This is exactly what Jack does. He is a representative of the majority of people.

But "Jack" does two things that I suppose most people who share his intuitions do not bother to do. First, he searches for an explanation of why he finds the "logic" of sure-thing reasoning compelling, in the sense that he cannot figure out what is wrong with it, despite his contrary intuitions. Second, he searches for arguments that can justify, as rational, the non-sure-thing answers his intuitions tell him are correct.

Jack's explanation why he finds it so hard to find a flaw in sure-thing inferences (and Tamara's explanation) is that by using one of the clauses of Principle B as the leading principle of an inference, it is natural for any person contemplating the inference to parse it into distinct "logical modules." When the person thinks about one of these logical modules in isolation from the others, he is strongly inclined to interpret the meanings of the sentences in that module in such a way that the reasoning expressed by the module is valid. The person does this by adopting a certain "epistemic perspective," for example, the perspective of e_1, as opposed to e_2 (in the terminology of Principle B). But then, when the person considers a different logical module, also in isolation, he adopts a different epistemic perspective, one that will make the reasoning of *that* module valid. Since a sentence may occur in more than one logical module, this leads to a fallacious shifting of perspective, but one hardly noticed by the reasoner.

Tamara brings this out by having Casey break his sure-thing arguments into logical modules in just this way when he presents the arguments to Jack. It was Tamara's view that Casey, as much as Jack, was being misled by these subtle changes in epistemic perspective. She thought that, at least in the cases she considers, proponents of sure-thing reasoning are proponents because they are tricking themselves with a subtle equivocation. Her goal in these parts of "The Backtracking Fallacy" is to show why this is the "natural"—meaning the human—way to think.

The second thing Jack does is work out reasons why his non-sure-thing intuitions are rationally defensible. He does this by articulating "policies" for solving certain types of decision problem, policies that can conflict with the policy of *always* accepting the result of a sure-thing inference. All of these policies are optional, in the sense that a decision-maker might, rationally, follow the policy, or might, rationally, decline to follow it.

Tamara's point (Jack's point) is that by allowing flexibility in one's choice of decision-making policies, one may have to abandon the idea of having a single, widely applicable, "logic" for making certain kinds of decision. But one gains the ability to let many alternative values have equal (though not obligatory) force in practical deliberation.

In "Stipulation and Epistemological Privilege," Tamara argues against the claim that when the meaning of a term is "stipulated," this provides a basis for a priori knowledge: For example, if A is stipulated to mean F, one can know a priori that A is F by attending to the stipulation. What is especially interesting is her argument against a subtle variation on this claim that was first described and defended by Saul Kripke in "Naming and Necessity."[8]

A little background will help. Kripke takes proper names to be "rigid designators"—they denote the same object in every possible world in which that object exists. A person can "fix the reference" of a name by using a description that applies uniquely to the intended referent, even when (as is typically the case) the description does not fit the object in some possible worlds in which the object exists.

It will be helpful to have an example that slightly simplifies the allegedly "a priori" knowledge Tamara discusses, since the simplification will affect nothing of substance. Suppose unexplained perturbations are observed in the orbits of certain planets. An astronomer reasons that these perturbations could be explained by positing another, unobserved, planet, which causes the perturbations. She accepts this hypothesis, and names the posited planet 'Neptune'—fixing the reference of this name by means of the description "the planet causing the perturbations." There are some philosophical lessons to be learned from such examples, Kripke believes. For instance, the following sentence expresses a contingent proposition, not a necessary one:

> (N) If Neptune exists, then Neptune is the planet causing the perturbations.

That is because if 'Neptune' has been introduced successfully as a denoting name, then there are possible worlds (possible sets of circumstances) in which the object Neptune exists, but something "nonplanetary" causes the perturbations (or perhaps several planets in conjunction are the cause). Nevertheless, the astronomer can know (N) a priori "in the vicinity of" her "baptism" of Neptune as "the planet causing the perturbations." The idea is that she can reason: "Either I have failed to name anything 'Neptune' because my hypothesis is wrong, in which case (N) is true by falsity of its antecedent, or else my hypothesis is right, and once again (N) is true. Since the description fixing the reference of 'Neptune' has exactly the content 'the planet causing the perturbations,' I can be sure there is no way for the antecedent of (N) to be true except by having the consequent of (N) true as well." The astonishing conclusion is that a person can have a priori knowledge of a contingent proposition.

Tamara gives two different arguments against this position. One seems to me unconvincing, but the other is very convincing and as subtle as the position it refutes. I will simplify both of her arguments (as I simplified Kripke's claim). I think my simplifications will not misrepresent the arguments.

One of Tamara's arguments goes this way. Suppose things are as in Kripke's story. But many years pass, Neptune is observed telescopically, visited by spacecraft, colonized. We learn a great deal about it. Finally, we learn that the laws of planetary mechanics are very different from what the astronomer supposed them to be. Neptune never caused the perturbations; they were caused in some other way. We say that (N) is false, was false when the astronomer first considered it, and therefore was not something she *knew*. So she did not know it a priori, since she did not know it at all.

I do not think Kripke should accept this argument. What happens in Tamara's story is that our linguistic community gradually evolves a much more complicated description of Neptune than the description used by the astronomer to fix the reference of the name. If "we," at this much later time, were asked to *describe* Neptune, we would not give as our description "the planet causing the perturbations." But it remains true that the astronomer did use that description. Presumably, one of Kripke's reasons for restricting his claim that the astronomer has a priori knowledge in the temporal neighborhood of the "baptism" was to emphasize that descriptions of Neptune that might later be generally accepted as correct should not be tacitly substituted for the description the astronomer actually used.

Tamara's second argument is in the form of a dilemma. Assume first that the astronomer is introducing the name 'Neptune' into a public language, such as English. There are, she assumes, criteria a person must satisfy in order to be "licensed" to name a new planet. Perhaps these criteria include having discovered the planet in some sense of 'discover'.

Perhaps the criteria are quite complex. Whatever these criteria are, it will be an empirical matter whether a person satisfies them. Nobody, the astronomer included, can know a priori that the astronomer satisfies these criteria. Therefore, the astronomer cannot know a priori that (N) is true, because she cannot know a priori that she is entitled to name a planet 'Neptune'. Perhaps the astronomer's attempt at fixing the reference of 'Neptune' is an idle gesture, because she is not qualified to fix the reference of 'Neptune', whereas someone else who is qualified fixes the reference in such a way that 'Neptune' denotes a planet that does not fit the description in the consequent of (N). Then (N) would be false. We can assume that the astronomer does know—a posteriori—that she is entitled to fix the reference of 'Neptune' as she does. But this cannot lead her to a priori knowledge of (N).

Now assume that the astronomer does not intend to introduce the name 'Neptune' into the public language. She merely intends to introduce it into her private idiolect. Maybe she need not satisfy any "licensing" criteria to do that. Maybe she just needs to choose to do it. But it remains true that her attempt at reference fixing must possess certain properties in order to be successful, properties one cannot know a priori are present.

Tamara's examples are convincing (and funny). She imagines someone manically "naming" some object first one thing, then another, then another, in a sequence so fast that at no time does the person settle even briefly into a stable name-use. If a person behaves this way, she does not succeed in naming the object. If the astronomer is behaving in this way, she does not succeed in fixing the reference of 'Neptune' even for her private, idiolectic, use of language. Of course she knows she is not behaving this way, but she only knows it empirically.

This still is not quite enough. If the only problem the astronomer needs to worry about is that she has not named *anything* 'Neptune', she can know (N) a priori, since she knows that (N) is true if its antecedent is false. But the astronomer has to worry about more than that. She must know *whether or not* she has gone about her attempt at reference fixing in a sufficiently "orderly" way to name anything 'Neptune', *and if so, what,* and *how* (with what description) she has fixed the reference. These questions, too, she can answer only empirically—though of course she can answer them *easily* empirically. I take this point to be implicit in Tamara's argument.

So, on both horns of the dilemma, the astronomer fails to know a priori that he has fixed the reference of 'Neptune' as "the one planet causing the perturbations." And this follows even when we consider the knowledge the astronomer can have in the vicinity of the baptism.

In "Newcomb's Problem as a Thought Experiment," Tamara gives a detailed illustration of a problem she believed common to most "thought experiments" in philosophy. Since the example she chooses in this essay is a thought experiment in decision theory, I'll give a brief account of the problem she is worried about as it occurs in decision theory.

In a typical thought experiment in decision theory, a hypothetical situation is described in which a choice must be made between two or more possible actions. The thought-experimenter "thinks herself into" the hypothetical situation, decides which possible action she would choose, and then asks whether this choice tends to support the plausibility of one theory of rational choice as compared with others. Tamara's concern is that the hypothetical situation always is described *schematically*. Normative features of the hypothetical situation are stipulated. The decision-maker is said to "know" some things but not others; certain probabilities are said to be those he should ascribe to various events; certain results are said to be more desirable than, or preferred to, others. Usually only the sketchiest information is included about *how* the decision-maker has acquired this knowledge, or arrived at these probabilities, or come to have these desires and preferences. Usually very little effort is made to show that these normative properties could be possessed by a real person in real circumstances, and—in particular—that these stipulated normative properties are compatible with the (also stipulated) nonnormative properties of the hypothetical decision-maker in the hypothetical situation.

One can take a "schema" of this sort and fill in the missing details to one extent or another. Tamara calls these somewhat-filled-in hypothetical situations "realizations." Often, perhaps always, a given schema can be realized in very different ways, the differences being such as to alter the thought-experimenter's considered opinion as to what choices would be correct. Tamara was convinced that this problem of multiple realizations of schematically described hypothetical situations—perhaps leading to incompatible "outcomes" of the thought experiment—was one of the main defects of the method of thought experimentation in decision theory and in philosophy generally.

I will summarize Tamara's argument in this essay very briefly, and urge the reader to turn instead to her own richly detailed discussion. This is her description of Newcomb's problem, and her initial comment on "realizing" it:

> "Newcomb's problem" asks what we should do if the following events took place: A mysterious extraterrestrial being descends and astounds us for a while with various exhibitions of inhuman intellectual prowess. As a curtain-closing act, the Being leaves a pair of boxes for each adult human, one transparent and containing a thousand dollars and one opaque. The Being announces that it has predicted what each of us will do when, as has been scheduled, we choose to take either the contents of both boxes or the contents only of the opaque box. On the basis of these predictions, the Being has placed a million dollars in someone's opaque box if the person will choose just that box, and nothing in the opaque box if the person will choose both boxes. As time goes by, many thousands of people make choices, and the Being's rate of successful prediction is very high, around 90 percent (about nine of ten one-boxers have found a million, and nine out of ten two-boxers have found only the obvious thousand). "Our" time has come to choose.
>
> The Newcomb problem stipulates that (I) we know that a superior Being has made predictions about our choices far into the future and arranged money in boxes accordingly. It also stipulates that (II) we know a fair amount about the outcome of people making their choices but (III) we do not understand the causal processes that lead to these outcomes. I will argue that there is no way to realize the three stipulations of this thought experiment schema while at the same time having a thought experiment that is relevant to the theory of rational choice.[9]

The two realizations Tamara discusses can be described, roughly, as (1) the way people resembling us in epistemic norms, and reasonably well-informed, would actually assess the hypothetical situation in Newcomb's problem (or rather, what such people would believe the situation really was); and (2) the way people like us in some respects, though very unlike us in others, would assess the hypothetical situation.

Tamara's conclusion about realization (1) is that "we" would believe some method existed for telling, at about the time box-choices were going to be made by a person, what that person was going to do. We would not buy the predicting-being story. So, condition (I) mentioned in the passage quoted here would not be satisfied in this realization. "Our" most plausible approach to the choice problem would be what Tamara calls an "indirect strategy." In this case, we should steadfastly set ourselves to take one box, on the assumption that by so doing we will do something (we don't know what) that "triggers" the placing of a million dollars in the million-dollar box.

Tamara's conclusion about realization (2) relies on some assumptions about the cultural and psychological traits that would be required for people to actually believe the predicting-being story. (She calls them the "Gullibles"). The Gullibles satisfy all three conditions, (I), (II), and (III), she mentions. But, she argues, we cannot become Gullibles, except perhaps by gradual cultural evolution. The difference between our epistemic norms and Gullible epistemic norms is too great for their norms to be an option for us. She adds that "theories of rational decision need only stand testing in hypothetical situations that *we* can confront."[10]

When we try to realize the schema, we find that there is no realization that both satisfies conditions (I), (II), and (III) and qualifies as a situation in which theories of rational choice should be tested.

In "Making Rational Choices When Preferences Cycle," Tamara considers what decision-makers should do when they have preferences over a set of possible actions that are nontransitive in a cycling structure. Suppose the possible actions are A, B, C, and D. And suppose the person who must decide what to do has preferences as follows (where "M Pref N" means the person prefers doing M to doing N):

A Pref B, B Pref C, C Pref D, D Pref A.

Classical expected utility theory has an answer: The person should somehow alter her preferences so as to eliminate the cycle and restore transitivity. Some proponents of the classical theory have maintained that cyclic preferences are as irrational as contradictory beliefs. It is not hard to see why someone might think preference cycles are inherently irrational. The person whose preferences over actions A, B, C, and D form a cycle seems to be unable to choose any of the four actions without thereby choosing an action to which she prefers some *other* action.

Tamara believed that a person can have very good reasons for having some cyclic sets of preferences. Her aim in this essay was threefold: first, to argue that cyclic preferences can be rational; second, to rebut some frequently accepted arguments that it never can be rational to allow one's preferences to cycle; third, to describe some policies for decision-making that are plausible theories of rational choice, but tolerate preference cycles.

I will make just the following comment: One of the policies for making rational choices when preferences cycle is SSB utility theory, developed by Peter Fishburn.[11] This theory raises philosophical issues that are interesting quite apart from the theory's ability to provide a decision-maker with a coherent method for figuring out what to do in the presence of cyclic preferences.

To simplify greatly, SSB utility theory allows the decision-maker to choose from an expanded set of possible actions. For example, the person with the preference cycle over A, B, C, and D could also consider the action "$1/4A + 1/4B + 1/4C + 1/4D$," where this is understood to mean "acting so as to have a $1/4$ chance of doing A, a $1/4$ chance of doing B, a $1/4$ chance of doing C, and a $1/4$ chance of doing D." An infinite set of these "probabilistically mixed" actions are added to the alternatives open to the decision-maker (subject to a few simple constraints).

Tamara thinks of the decision-maker as using a randomizing device, for example, a spinner marked off in quadrants labeled "A," "B," "C," and "D." The person spins the spinner and performs whichever of A, B, C, or D the pointer indicates when the spinner stops. This is how one performs the action "$1/4A + 1/4B + 1/4C + 1/4D$." The theoretical strength of SSB utility theory is that even when every "normal" action in a set is dispreferred to some other action in the set, it can happen that there is one of these mixed actions to which nothing is preferred.

But—when the spinner stops, the decision-maker must follow through by performing whichever "unmixed" act the spinner indicates, and since there is a preference cycle over these unmixed acts, the decision-maker prefers some other act to that one. Is it rational to "follow through" in this way? The reader can study Tamara's arguments that it is rational, and decide.

Tamara's "Philosophical Intuitions and Psychological Theory" is the only essay in this collection that does rely heavily, in its main argument, on the strategy of using scientific theory to rebut a philosophical argument. Philosophers sometimes perform thought experiments that lead them to have firm intuitions as to which possible answer to a philosophical question is the correct answer. In the same "act of thought" the philosopher intuits the philosophical principle he is applying in arriving at his answer. Finally, the philosopher concludes that this thought experiment has provided some measure of credibility, a priori, to both the answer and the philosophical principle.

Tamara's thesis in this essay is that the second intuitive judgment—the judgment as to what principle is guiding the intuitive choice of correct answer—can be completely wrong without the philosopher having any cognitive access to the fact that it is completely wrong.

The thought experiment Tamara uses as a case study is in the late Warren Quinn's "Actions, Intentions, and Consequences: The Doctrine of Doing and Allowing."[12] Quinn's brief summary of the Doctrine of Doing and Allowing is ". . . others deny that consequences are the only things of moral relevance. To them it matters whether the harm comes from action, for example from killing someone, or from inaction, for example from not saving someone. They hold that for some good ends we may properly allow some evil to befall someone, even though we could not actively bring that evil about.".[13]

Quinn's thought experiment asks what the morally correct action would be in each of two hypothetical situations, as follows.

> Rescue Dilemma 1: We can either save five people in danger of drowning in one place or a single person in danger of drowning somewhere else. We cannot save all six.
> Rescue Dilemma 2: We can save the five only by driving over and thereby killing someone who (for an unspecified reason) is trapped on the road. If we do not undertake the rescue the trapped person can later be freed.[14]

Tamara's summary of Quinn's report of the outcome of this thought experiment is as follows.

> Quinn's intuition is that in Rescue Dilemma 1 we are perfectly justified in saving the group of five people, even though we thereby fail to save the solitary person, whereas in Rescue Dilemma 2 it is "far from obvious that we *may* proceed." In his discussion, he reports that the intuitions of some other philosophers match his own. And he seems to think it likely that the reader will have intuitions that match his own. For the purposes of this article, I shall assume Quinn is right about this widespread similarity of intuitions.[15]

Tamara continues:

> Quinn appears to assume that anyone who responds to these cases as he
> does has moral intuitions, which, like his, conform to the Doctrine of
> Doing and Allowing. After trying several formulations of this doctrine,
> he writes: "Perhaps we have found the basic form of the doctrine and the
> natural qualifications that, when combined with other plausible moral
> principles, accurately map our moral intuitions." Quinn then goes on to
> develop a philosophical defense of the doctrine. I am not concerned here
> with whether or not there is a philosophical defense of the Doctrine of
> Doing and Allowing. I am concerned instead with Quinn's assumption
> that people who share his intuitions in the case of Rescue Dilemma 1
> and Rescue Dilemma 2 do so because they accept, however inexplicitly,
> the Doctrine of Doing and Allowing. Indeed, I am concerned with
> Quinn's assumption that he himself has these intuitions because
> he (antecedently) accepts the Doctrine of Doing and Allowing. The
> ground for my concern is that it might be the case, rather, that Quinn has
> these intuitions as a result of covert reasoning of the kind posited by
> prospect theory. If this is the best explanation, then Quinn is wrong to
> think of these intuitions as the product of a very different pattern of
> reasoning involving a distinction between doing and allowing.[16]

Tamara's suggestion is that the widely shared intuitions with respect
to the two rescue dilemmas should be given a psychological explanation
that differs significantly from an explanation in terms of the relative
moral acceptability of killing and letting die. The following very simplified version of her preferred explanation will make the difference clear
(though it is *so* simplified that it is unfair both to Quinn and to Tamara).

When a decision-maker is considering a decision problem involving
gains or losses, she chooses a "status quo" from which the gains or losses
are measured. The language in which the problem is expressed can influence this choice of a status quo. In Rescue Dilemma 1, the thought
experimenter chooses as a status quo the situation in which the "sixth
person" dies, so that a decision to save the person corresponds to an increase in value, a positive movement along a curve graphing "psychologically real" value against units of some "good," in this case, lives. In
Rescue Dilemma 2, the thought experimenter chooses as a status quo the
situation in which the "sixth person" lives, so that a decision to kill that
person corresponds to a decrease in value, a negative movement along the
curve.

Empirical research has shown that the shape of a person's "value curve" is different for the part of the curve in a positive direction from a chosen status quo, and for the part of the curve in a negative direction from a chosen status quo. The "positive" curve is concave and relatively shallow in (average) slope; the "negative" curve is convex and relatively steep in (average) slope. As a result, positive movements from a status quo "count for less" psychologically real value than do negative movements from a status quo.[17]

The thought experimenter considering Rescue Dilemma 1 regards "saving" the sixth person as a positive movement along a value curve from a status quo, whereas the thought experimenter considering Rescue Dilemma 2 regards "killing" the sixth person as a negative movement along a value curve from *another* status quo, because of the change in status quo point. So the "psychologically real value" of a life is *perceived* differently by the thought experimenter for the two rescue dilemmas. It may help to compare the graphs in chapter 6, 174–5.

This, Tamara argues, is what explains the difference in intuition from one Rescue Dilemma to the other. The Doctrine of Doing and Allowing is not a part of this explanation. But the thought experimenter's computation of psychologically real value is not something of which she is aware. So she feels free to seek a plausible explanation for her intuitions, and settles on the Doctrine of Doing and Allowing.

In order for Tamara's argument to be be an objection to Quinn's use of thought experiments, he must hold that one's belief in the Doctrine of Doing and Allowing *explains* one's intuitions, and he must hold that the existence of this explanation counts as grounds for accepting the Doctrine of Doing and Allowing. Then Tamara can assert, plausibly, that the different explanation she suggests has better empirical credentials. But a philosopher might insist that the Doctrine of Doing and Allowing is not put forward as a psychological explanation of the intuitions. Someone who replies in this way must describe an alternative role for the thought experiment, and must describe an alternative connection between the intuitions and the Doctrine of Doing and Allowing.

In "The Backtracking Fallacy," Tamara has "Jack" enunciate and defend various decision-making policies, always put forward to "explain"—in *some* sense—intuitions that are in conflict with sure-thing reasoning. It is not clear to me to what extent Tamara intended "Jack's" explanations to be psychological explanations. If she did so intend them, then it seems to me she is open to a weaker form of the objection she makes against Quinn: If no empirical research shows that it is reasoning according to "Jack's" policies that in fact motivates people to have these particular non-sure-thing intuitions, then how can we be confident that the best psychological explanation does not invoke entirely different principles?

Notes

1. Chapter 3, 129.

2. Chapter 3, 129.

3. Chapter 3, 129.

4. Chapter 3, 133.

5. Chapter 3, 135–136.

6. Leonard Savage, *The Foundations of Statistics*, 2nd ed. (New York: Dover, 1972), 21.

7. Chapter 1, 64–65.

8. Saul Kripke, "Naming and Necessity," in *Semantics of Natural Languages*, ed. D. Davidson and G. Harman (Dordrecht: Reidel, 1972), 253–355.

9. Chapter 5, 155.

10. Chapter 5, 165.

11. Peter Fishburn, *Nonlinear Preference and Utility Theory* (Baltimore: Johns Hopkins University Press, 1988).

12. In *Morality and Action* (Cambridge: Cambridge University Press, 1993).

13. Quinn, *Morality and Action*, 149.

14. Chapter 6, 169.

15. Chapter 6, 169.

16. Chapter 6, 170.

17. See Tamara's references to the scientific literature, chapter 6, 170.

1

THE BACKTRACKING FALLACY

"Quasi"-Constructive Dilemmas

Generally, when someone must make a decision in the face of uncertainty, logic will not suffice. So an agent is fortunate if he can base such a decision upon a principle that is as acceptable, or almost as acceptable, as a principle of logic—a principle that can be counted on not to lead him astray and that can be certified a priori—but at the same time a principle that tells him how to act, not just how to think.

In his influential book *The Foundations of Statistics*, Leonard Savage proposed a set of principles to tell people what they ought to do when they want to act in their own self-interest as they see it. This set of principles constituted a version of "subjective expected utility theory": No choice can satisfy the principles unless it maximizes (or coequally maximizes) expected "utility," where the utility of an outcome for an agent is entirely determined by the agent's preferences, whether or not these preferences reflect what "really is" good for the agent, or what "really is" in the agent's self-interest.

Savage believed that the principles he proposed were indeed as acceptable, or almost as acceptable, as principles of logic. He believed they should be thought of as extending logic, in order to make it more usefully applicable in situations where uncertainty is present.[1] I want to focus on just one of Savage's principles: what he called the "sure-thing principle" (STP). Savage told a nice little story to illustrate STP in action:

> A businessman contemplates buying a certain piece of property. He
> considers the outcome of the next presidential election relevant to the

attractiveness of the purchase. So, to clarify the matter for himself, he asks whether he would buy if he knew that the Republican candidate were going to win, and he decides that he would do so. Similarly he considers whether he would buy if he knew that the Democratic candidate were going to win, and again finds that he would do so. Seeing that he would buy in either event, he decides that he should buy, even though he does not know which event obtains, or will obtain, as we would ordinarily say.[2]

Call this the Businessman Argument. The businessman does not know whether a Democrat or a Republican will win, so he must make a decision in the face of uncertainty. But despite this uncertainty, he is able to decide now, in his present state of knowledge, what his preference would be if he learned that a Democrat was going to be elected, and he is able to decide now, in his present state of knowledge, what his preference would be if learned that a Republican was going to be elected. Fortunately for him, he would have exactly the same preference regardless of which piece of information he received. It is a "sure thing" that once he learns the election results he will prefer buying the property to passing up the chance; so he concludes that the right choice for him to make now, before he learns the results, in fact before he can make any reasonable prediction what the results will be, is to go ahead and buy the property.

The businessman's reasoning bears at least a superficial resemblance to one of the valid forms of argument recognized by classical logic: "constructive dilemma." A constructive dilemma has the form:

Either A or not A.
If A, then B.
If not A, then B.
Therefore, B.

A and B may be any sentences. So an example of constructive dilemma is:

Either Jack did it or it is not the case that Jack did it.
If Jack did it, he'll act guilty.
If it is not the case that Jack did it, he'll act guilty anyway.
So, Jack will act guilty.

In this discussion I will count as constructive dilemmas certain arguments that fall just short of fitting the traditional definition; for instance:

Either Jack did it or he didn't.
If Jack did it, he'll act guilty.
If Jack didn't do it, he'll act guilty anyway.
So, Jack will act guilty.

A perfectionist could insist that the first premise of this argument does not have the form "A or not A," since both "Jack did it" and "Jack didn't do it" imply that that there is such a person as Jack, whereas, strictly speaking, "Either Jack did it or it is not the case that Jack did it" does not have that implication; it would be true even in a situation where Jack did not exist. I will not be a perfectionist; in this discussion arguments like the second "Jack" argument will count as constructive dilemmas, to avoid the strained locution "it is not the case that" whenever possible.

The Businessman Argument is not a constructive dilemma even by the informal standard I am using. For one thing, the businessman is trying to decide what to do, not what to think. His conclusion is to the effect that it would be rational of him to buy a piece of property; or perhaps that it would be rational of him to prefer buying it to not buying it. So the Businessman Argument is an example of "practical reasoning," not an example of "theoretical reasoning," to borrow some standard jargon. Second, the businessman is deciding what it would be rational of him to prefer now, in his present state of knowledge, by seeing what it would be rational of him to prefer if he were to receive information he does not now possess. He reasons that there are only two pieces of information he needs to worry about—"the Democrat will win (or has won)" and "the Republican will win (or has won)." He is bound to receive one or the other of these pieces of information. Whichever of these pieces of information he receives, he will be in a new state of knowledge, importantly different from his present state of knowledge. If he were in either of these new states of knowledge, he would then *prefer to have bought* the property. He concludes that it is rational for him to prefer to buy the property now, in his present state of knowledge.

Classical logic does not contain principles that tell us what is rational to prefer in one state of knowledge on the basis of what it would be rational to prefer in other, as yet unrealized, states of knowledge. In fact, the schematic form of constructive dilemma I presented earlier makes no reference at all to "knowledge." Savage knew this, and did not say that the Businessman Argument is a constructive dilemma. But intuitively, the Businessman Argument is persuasive precisely because it shares with constructive dilemmas the property that the conclusion has been shown to be a "sure thing"—however things develop, the conclusion should be accepted. I will call arguments like the Businessman Argument "quasi"-constructive dilemmas (QCDs). A hallmark of QCDs is that they make reference to the reasoner's state of knowledge, though the reference may not be on the surface of the argument's language.

The new principle of reasoning Savage thought was at work in the Businessman Argument, the sure-thing principle, includes a reference to the reasoner's state of knowledge—at least in Savage's first, informal statements of it.[3] The following principle of reasoning, though simpler than the sure-thing principle, will suffice through the early part of this discussion as a working version of the principle Savage recommended.

> *Principle P:* If someone should prefer having performed act g to having performed act f, either knowing that the event B obtained or knowing that the event not-B obtained, then the person should prefer g to f in fact (that is, before learning whether B or not-B obtains).

It does seem that Principle P captures the "logic" of the businessman's reasoning. And Principle P does seem to be unimpeachable. But these are first impressions. Will they hold up under close examination? How, exactly, does one identify the principle of reasoning somebody is following? And how, exactly, does one tell whether a given principle of reasoning is acceptable? We must try to answer both questions, at least in the special case of "sure-thing" reasoning.

Underdetermination of Form

Suppose two friends, Jack and Casey, are having their daily philosophical chat as they stroll around the park. As usual, Casey tries to persuade Jack to accept some argument, and as usual Jack balks, but cannot explain why. This time the argument turns on what is sometimes called a "quantifier order confusion." Casey's argument goes as follows.

The Chimp Argument
(1) There is a chimp stronger than any man.
(2) John is a man and so is David.
Therefore,
(3) There is a chimp stronger than John and also stronger than David.

Since John and David are the strongest men Jack and Casey know, the conclusion of the Chimp Argument disturbs Jack a good deal. But Casey defends the Chimp Argument with a two-part defense. First he argues that the first premise is true. He asks, "If you took any man, and tested his strength against a series of chimps, don't you think, sooner or later, you would find a chimp who is stronger than he is?" Jack agrees that what Casey has said makes sense. The second premise is obviously true; it says that John and David are men. Then, having convinced Jack of the premises, Casey claims that in the Chimp Argument the conclusion follows from the premises by the following perfectly valid principle of reasoning:

> Principle Q: If there is a chimp, who bears the relation *stronger than* to any man, and if John and David are men, then there is a chimp who bears the relation *stronger than* to John and also bears the relation *stronger than* to David.

Jack thinks about the pattern of reasoning of the Chimp Argument. It does seem to be an example of reasoning according to Principle Q. And Principle Q does seem valid. But something continues to bother Jack. He sees that the premises of the Chimp Argument are, or appear, true, just as Casey has said. And he sees that the argument appears to be an instance of Principle Q. And he sees that Principle Q is very compelling. But he has a sense that something is wrong with the Chimp Argument, even though he cannot put his finger on the problem. He declines to accept the conclusion, and he declines to accept the Chimp Argument as providing a good reason for its conclusion.

Of course, we can say what the problem is. Really there are two different principles of reasoning operative in Casey's presentation of the Chimp Argument:

> Principle Q⋆: If there is a chimp, who bears the relation *stronger than* to every man, and if John and David are men, then there is a chimp who bears the relation *stronger than* to John and also bears the relation *stronger than* to David.
>
> Principle Q⋆⋆: If, for every man, there is a chimp who bears the relation *stronger than* to that man, and if John and David are men, then there is a chimp who bears the relation *stronger than* to John and also bears the relation *stronger than* to David.

Casey's strategic choice of the phrase "any man" in premise (1) of the Chimp Argument, and in Principle Q, blurred the distinction between the quantifier order "there is ... every" in the antecedent of Principle Q⋆ and the quantifier order "every ... there is" in the antecedent of Principle Q⋆⋆. Casey's defense of the Chimp Argument turns on this conflation. In order to persuade Jack that premise (1) of the argument is true, he gives that premise the following interpretation:

> (1⋆⋆) For every man, there is a chimp who bears the relation *stronger than* to that man.

If Casey had given premise (1) the interpretation:

> (1⋆) There is a chimp, who bears the relation *stronger than* to every man

Jack might have resisted. He might have asked where this mighty chimp lives, what it is named, and so forth. But in order to reason from the premises (1⋆⋆) and (2) to the conclusion (3), one needs to use Principle Q⋆⋆. This principle is very unlikely to be true.

Principle Q⋆, on the other hand, is logically valid; one can know a priori that it is true. But in order for the conclusion (3) to follow from the premises (1) and (2) according to Principle Q⋆, premise (1) must be given the implausible interpretation (1⋆). So the Chimp Argument either has true premises but a faulty principle of reasoning, or a faultless principle of reasoning and a false premise. Casey is able to disguise this situation up to a point by presenting Jack with Principle Q. Given the actual wording of the Chimp Argument, Principle Q seems to give an accurate description of the "form" of the argument. When Casey wants Jack to accept Principle

Q, he tries to interpret it as Principle Q⋆. But when he wants Jack to accept premise (1), he switches to the other "quantifier order."

Jack is dimly, one might say implicitly, aware that a trick is being played. So he is not convinced by the Chimp Argument. But he cannot articulate what the trick is. This is not an implausible little story, actually. In the early to middle nineteenth century, able mathematicians were unable to articulate quantifier order distinctions hidden within such concepts as "continuous function."

It will be helpful to have some terminology for situations like this one. So, let us say that Principle Q is the *apparent* principle of reasoning operative in the Chimp Argument. Principle Q⋆ and Principle Q⋆⋆ are the *underlying* principles of reasoning operative in the Chimp Argument. The language of the Chimp Argument, the "surface" of the argument, underdetermines one's choice of underlying principle of reasoning. So it is possible to "hear" the argument either way, or perhaps both ways at once, without realizing one is doing this. Casey's sophistical attempt to convince Jack to accept the Chimp Argument makes use of this fact.

It will be my goal in this book to argue that many quasi-constructive dilemmas have more than one underlying principle of reasoning, underdetermined by the surface form of the argument. When a principle of reasoning is simply "read off of" the face of the words of a QCD, as is the case with Principle P, the principle one arrives at often will be an apparent principle only. But it may seem to describe perfectly the reasoning of the argument, just as the apparent Principle Q seemed to Jack to describe perfectly the reasoning of the Chimp Argument.

The underlying principles of reasoning operative in a QCD exhibit more of the argument's structure than does the apparent principle of reasoning, just as Principles Q⋆ and Q⋆⋆ exhibit more of the structure of the Chimp Argument than is exhibited by Principle Q (they exhibit enough structure to distinguish quantifier order). Sometimes both underlying principles of reasoning for a QCD are very compelling; sometimes both are very implausible; sometimes one underlying principle is compelling but the other is implausible. At least so I believe, and so I hope to show.

If my view is right, one would expect that at least sometimes people feel disinclined to accept a QCD, even if they have a hard time saying why they shouldn't accept it, considering that the conclusion is a "sure thing." And that is exactly what happens, as the reader can see by putting another little story alongside Savage's story of the businessman.

The Lawyer Argument

Here is the new story.

> In a criminal trial a defense attorney argues to the jury that her client
> either didn't do it, or else is insane, since the horrific nature of the
> crime bespeaks insanity. She goes on to argue that if the jury had con-
> vincing proof that her client didn't do it, they would, of course, decide
> to acquit. If, on the other hand, they had convincing proof that he did
> do it, they would have no choice but to acquit him on grounds of
> insanity. Therefore, they should decide to acquit him, without having
> proof either way.[4]

Now, juries in the United States today usually do not acquit on insanity grounds when the crime is serious. Moreover, juries are not permitted to reach verdicts until evidence has been put before them (though
of course they do), and lawyers are not permitted to urge juries to violate
this requirement (though of course they do). But attempt the thought
experiment of putting yourself in the position of a juror who has been
given this argument. While you do this, adopt the policy of acquitting the
insane (perhaps so that they can be held in secure mental health facilities).
And ignore the *legal* requirement that you make no decision until all
evidence is in. If you are like me, and like most people I have asked about
this example, you will find it abhorrent to make a weighty decision about
the life or the freedom of another person without evidence of the person's
guilt or innocence. The lawyer's "second-level" argument, resting as it
does on the (assumed) fact that actual "first-level" evidence can be—
indeed will be—obtained, will not have the same weight for you as "first-
level" evidence itself. Even if you stipulate that eventually you are going to
be presented with absolutely compelling evidence of guilt, or absolutely
compelling evidence of innocence, you will insist on waiting for that
evidence to be in your hands before making your decision.

But the Lawyer Argument (as I'll call it) is another QCD. As is the
case with the Businessman Argument, the principle of reasoning operative in the Lawyer Argument appears to be:

> *Principle P:* If someone should prefer having performed act g to having
> performed act f, either knowing that the event B obtained or knowing
> that the event not-B obtained, then the person should prefer g to f in
> fact (that is, before learning whether B or not-B obtains).

Principle P still sounds good, but in this case the argument is un-convincing. Imagine the lawyer trying to persuade you, just as Casey tried to persuade Jack about the chimp. The lawyer says: "Look, there are only two ways it can come out, as you surely agree. Either proof of my client's innocence will be forthcoming, or proof of his guilt will be forthcoming (we'll stipulate that no other outcomes are really possible). Either way it comes out, you will be sitting there convinced you should acquit my client. So why wait? Do it now." This sounds good. Some jurors might give in, unable to see how to rebut the lawyer's "logic." But others (I would be one) would continue to have a strong intuition that the argument should be rejected. It is not hard to imagine a juror's mistrust of lawyers as silver-tongued devils being confirmed.

The correct explanation of the "logical dynamics" of the Lawyer Argument may not parallel the correct explanation in the case of the Chimp Argument, but the similarities are striking. Later I will work through a different example in detail, and will do so again further on. Each time a bit more of the picture will get clear.

But in all of these cases I will need to rely heavily on "intuitions" about the goodness or badness of certain pieces of reasoning. If one is a philosopher, or any other sort of theoretician with a vested interest in the outcome of these "intuitive thought experiments," it is wise to compare one's intuitions with the inferential choices made by people who have no theoretical axes to grind, at least in a few cases.[5] So, let's pause to look at a pair of psychological experiments (or a pair of groups of experi-ments) in which most subjects reject QCD reasoning, with a minority of subjects accepting it. I take it that the analysis I intend to develop is required to make sense of *both* responses.[6]

Hawaii Vacations

The psychological experiments I describe here will pop up again later, to help me make several different points. Here they are intended only to drive home the fact that in a number of cases in which theoretically unbiased experimental subjects are confronted with reasoning that appears to obey Principle P, a significant number of subjects decline to accept the reasoning.[7]

I will call the two (groups of) experiments the "Hawaii vacation experiment" and the "sequential coin toss experiment."[8] In the first experiment, the subjects were given the following instructions:

> Imagine that you have just taken a tough qualifying examination. It is the end of the fall quarter and you feel tired and rundown, and you are not sure that you passed the exam. If you failed, you will have to take the exam again in a couple of months—after the Christmas holidays. You now have an opportunity to buy a very attractive five-day Christmas vacation package to Hawaii at an exceptionally low price. The special offer expires tomorrow, while the exam grade will not be available until the following day.

Call this the "Don't Know" version of the problem. After being presented with this version of the problem, the subjects are then asked the following questions: "Would you buy the vacation package?" "Would you not buy the package?" or: "Would you pay a $5 non-refundable fee in order to retain the right to buy the vacation package at the same exceptional price the day after tomorrow—after you find out whether or not you passed the exam?" When faced with these questions in the "Don't Know" version of the problem, most subjects preferred to pay the $5 fee, in order to postpone their decision until they had learned the exam results. (We assume that a $5 fee was a meaningful "cost" for these subjects; had all the subjects been billionaires, or Buddhist monks who had no attachment to money, an adjustment in the terms of the experiment would have been required.)

Two additional versions of the problem, called "Pass" and "Fail," were presented to two different groups of subjects. In the "Pass" version, the subjects are told they already have learned they passed the exam, and in the "Fail" version the subjects are told they already have learned they failed the exam. In both the "Pass" and the "Fail" versions, most subjects preferred to buy the vacation package (immediately, there being no point to postponing the decision).[9]

In the sequential coin toss experiment, subjects were given the following instructions: imagine that you have just played a gamble that gave you a 50 percent chance to win $200 and a 50 percent chance to lose $100, and that you don't know whether you won or lost this gamble. Call this the "Don't Know" version. They were then asked whether they would play a second identical gamble. A solid majority of the subjects *rejected* the second gamble.

Two additional versions of this problem were presented to these subjects. In the "Won" version, they were asked to imagine that they have just played a gamble that gave them a 50 percent chance to win $200 and a 50 percent chance to lose $100, and that they won the $200. In this version, when they were asked whether, if they were offered a second identical gamble, they would accept or reject the second gamble, a solid majority said they would *accept* the second gamble. Later they were given the "Lost" version of the problem, where they were asked to imagine that they just played a gamble that gave them a 50 percent chance to win $200 and a 50 percent chance to lose $100, and that they lost $100 in this gamble. A solid majority said that they would *accept* the second gamble in this case as well.

Here we have the same pattern of results as in the Hawaiian vacation case. A solid majority of the subjects make one decision in both the "Won" and "Lost" versions but make the opposite decision in the "Don't Know" version.[10]

It appears from these experimental results that a significant number of people in the "Don't Know" situation with respect to the exam results in the Hawaii vacation setup should be expected to reject the argument:

(1) Either you will learn you passed or you will learn you failed. These are the only real possibilities.

(2) If you knew you passed, you would buy the vacation package immediately.

(3) Similarly, if you knew you failed, you would buy the vacation package immediately.

(4) Therefore, you should buy the vacation package immediately, and not waste five dollars buying the right to postpone your decision.

That is, a significant number of people should be expected to affirm (1), (2), and (3), while rejecting the conclusion (4). At the same time, some people should be expected to affirm (4), having affirmed all the premises. The analogous point can be made about the sequential coin toss situation. A significant number of people in the "Don't Know" situation with respect to the bet should be expected to reject the argument:

> (5) Either you will learn you won the first time you played the bet or you will learn you lost. These are the only real possibilities.
> (6) If you knew you won, you would take the bet again.
> (7) Similarly, if you knew you lost, you would take the bet again.
> (8) Therefore, you should take the bet again.

That is, a significant number of people should be expected to accept all the premises (5), (6), and (7) but reject the conclusion (8). And some people should be expected to accept the conclusion, having accepted the premises.

Of course, these subjects are not decision theorists, thinking through the arguments (1)...(4) or (5)...(8) as thought experiments to test Principle P, or to test Savage's "sure-thing" principle. The subjects may have had little grasp on what "principle of inference" was tacitly motivating their decision-making. Obviously, Principle P is not somehow displayed in the description of the problem the subjects are asked to solve. One might wonder what would happen if these subjects were induced to think about the structure of their reasoning. Later I will discuss the issues that arise when people are confronted with the fact that they have failed to conform to Principle P.

Theorists who are committed to the view that reasoning in accordance with Principle P is rationally required look for factors that would explain why the same incorrect response is produced so often.[11] If this is the right view to take, we can reformulate it this way. The aforementioned QCDs (1)...(4) and (5)...(8) ought to be accepted as compelling arguments—they ought to be seen as "nearly" valid. But some people, indeed a substantial number of people, would reject both of these arguments. So we need an explanation for this astonishing deviation from inferential rationality.

My view is different. I do not believe that it is rationally compulsory to accept the QCDs (1)...(4) and (5)...(8), and I do not believe it is rationally compulsory to accept certain other QCDs. A person could have epistemic policies that undercut certain QCDs; policies that are "optionally rational"—one need not follow them, but one also could have fully rational grounds for following them. What I need to be able to explain is different. Sure-thing reasoning—that is, QCDs—can seem irrefutable even to a person whose epistemic policies do not oblige him to accept the arguments in question. Such a person may feel the same dissonance Jack felt when Casey presented him with the Chimp Argument and then glossed it in a way that made it seem irrefutable. Jack felt "intuitively" that there was something wrong with the argument, but he couldn't put his finger on the flaw.

I will argue that in general when this occurs, the argument really has more "logical structure" than is revealed by Principle P. In part, my explanation will appeal to the way a person can shift back and forth between the underlying principles of reasoning in a given QCD, often without realizing that any such shift is occurring. That is what Jack was doing with the Chimp Argument. To illustrate how this "shifting" can occur in a QCD, let us return to Savage, and his defense of the sure-thing principle. In particular, let us focus on a QCD Savage devised in the course of rebutting an objection to his theory of rational choice, an objection known as the "Allais Problem."

Savage's Thought Experiment

Savage suggested the following method for deciding what is an acceptable principle of reasoning, or of decision-making, and what isn't.

> [W]hen certain maxims are presented for your consideration, you must
> ask yourself whether you try to behave in accordance with them, or, to
> put it differently, how you would react if you noticed yourself vio-
> lating them.[12]

As it happened, Savage was familiar with a thought experiment
called the "Allais Problem."[13] This thought experiment appears to refute
any set of practical principles that, like the set Savage recommends,
implies that every rational decision maximizes expected utility.[14]

The thought experiment has three steps. First consider a hypothetical situation, A1, in which you are offered a choice between two
gambles, G1 and G2, and decide which gamble you would accept;
second, consider a hypothetical situation, A2, in which you are offered a
choice between two gambles, G3 and G4, and decide which gamble you
would accept.

This is situation A1:

Choose between:
  G1:   Win $500,000 with probability 1.
and
  G2:   Win $2,500,000 with probability 0.10;
        win $500,000 with probability 0.89; and
        remain at the status quo with probability 0.01.

This is situation A2:

Choose between:
  G3:   Win $500,000 with probability 0.11;
        remain at the status quo with probability 0.89.
and
  G4:   Win $2,500,000 with probability 0.10;
        remain at the status quo with probability 0.90.

The third step in the thought experiment is a step of analysis of the
decisions reached in the first two steps. If you are like many people, you
will have chosen G1 in situation A1 and G4 in situation A2. You will have
reasoned in something like the following way. I prefer G1 to G2 because

I prefer to have $500,000 *for sure* to having a small (0.10) chance of getting $2,500,000, even when this small chance of getting $2,500,000 is packaged with a reasonably good, though less than certain, chance of gaining $500,000 (and a negligible chance of staying at the status quo). And you will have preferred G4 to G3 because you were not willing to give up a small 0.10 chance of gaining $2,500,000 in order to have a chance nearly as small (0.11) of getting only $500,000. This pair of decisions seems reasonable; that is, rationally acceptable though not rationally compulsory.

But this pattern of choices is inconsistent with your being an expected utility maximizer. This needs some explanation. First, a quick review of the idea of expected utility: In subjective expected utility theory, agents are conceived as having "utilities," or numerically expressible "ratings," of the various outcomes they contemplate their actions may have. Agents also are conceived of as expecting various outcomes of their actions with numerically expressible "subjective probabilities," or degrees of confidence. (Since subjective probabilities are just that, probabilities, they always are expressed by a real number in the range from 0 to 1, inclusive, where a subjective probability of 1 means absolute certainty.)

When the outcomes of several possible actions the agent contemplates satisfy a few "formal" conditions (e.g., the contemplated outcomes of a given possible action exhaust the class of possible outcomes of that action), then the agent can calculate an "expected utility" for each contemplated action as follows. Take the utility value attached to each possible outcome of a given possible action, "weight" this outcome for likelihood by multiplying the utility value by its subjective probability (conditional upon the agent performing the given possible action), and add the resulting weighted utility values for all of the possible outcomes of the given possible action. The result will be a "weighted value" for each possible action the agent is contemplating performing. These weighted values associated with a given possible action are standardly referred to as the "expected utilities" of the several possible actions.

According to subjective expective utility theory *taken as a descriptive thesis*, agents *do choose to perform* whichever contemplated action has the highest expected utility. According to subjective expected utility theory taken as a prescriptive, normative, thesis, agents *should perform* the action with highest expected utility, regardless of which action they actually do choose to perform. I always mean subjective expected utility theory

(SEUT) to be understood prescriptively. It is clear that in the argument under discussion, Savage also intends SEUT to be understood prescriptively—at least. He may also have intended SEUT to be understood descriptively—all at the same time—so he may have thought of the Allais experiment as possible empirical counterevidence to an empirical theory. If so, it is not this aspect of Savage's concern that I will be addressing.

Now, SEUT dictates that when you think about the proffered gambles G1, G2, G3, and G4, you (tacitly) assign utility values to the various possible outcomes. That is, you tacitly settle upon numbers U(\$2,500,000), U(\$500,000), and U(\$0). Strictly speaking, these should be written U(acquire \$2,500,000 more than you have), but I will write the utilities in simpler form, here and throughout, when the meaning is clear. Suppose you evaluate the various actions you are asked to contemplate performing—that is, the various bets you are asked to contemplate taking—by means of SEUT. You will first calculate the expected utilities of the four bets, and then you will compare the expected utilities. The expected utilities look like this:

G1 $(1.0)(U500,000)$
G2 $(0.10)(U2,500,000) + (0.89)(U500,000) + (0.01)(U0)$
G3 $(0.11)(U500,000) + (0.89)(U0)$
G4 $(0.10)(U2,500,000) + (0.90)(U0)$

Now, suppose you find yourself preferring G1 to G2, and preferring G4 to G3. Let $X=U2,500,000$, let $Y=U500,000$, and let $Z=U0$. If your preferences correspond to those of an expected utility maximizer, that is, if they agree with the dictates of SEUT, we have the inequalities:

$$(A) \quad (1.0)Y > (0.10)X + (0.89)Y + (0.01)Z$$

and

$$(B) \quad (0.10)X + (0.9)Z > (0.11)Y + (0.89)Z$$

Add the left side of (A) to the left side of (B), and the right side of (A) to the right side of (B). The result is:

$$(0.10)X + (1.0)Y + (0.9)Z > (0.10)X + (1.0)Y + (0.9)Z.$$

This is impossible, being of the form: $R > R$.

So you have found that you would choose among these hypothetical gambles in a way inconsistent with any set of practical principles

TABLE 1.1.   Savage's lottery style presentation.

Proffered gambles	Lottery ticket number		
	I	2–11	12–100
Situation A1			
G1	5	5	5
G2	0	25	5
Situation A2			
G3	5	5	0
G4	0	25	0
	(payoffs in 100,000 dollars)		

requiring that you maximize expected utility. Since Savage's principles are one such set, you have found that in some circumstances you would choose among alternative possible actions in a way that is inconsistent with Savage's principles.

In fact, Savage reports having performed this thought experiment himself and having decided that he preferred G1 and G4. But his response was not to rest content with this outcome. Instead, he took a step back from the choices among bets he intuitively preferred, and asked whether his choices might be an artifact of the way these bets were described in the thought experiment. Perhaps the formulation of these bets was in some way deceptive, concealing some element of their structure that, if revealed, would make it obvious that the opposite choice was correct. After a bit of reflection, he came to think that this is exactly what had happened.

The four gambles can be thought of as bets on a hundred-ticket lottery. For example, G2 can be thought of as a bet whereby you win nothing if ticket number 1 is drawn; you win $2,500,000 if one of the tickets 2 through 11 is drawn, and you win $500,000 if one of the tickets 12 through 100 is drawn. A bet like that would give you exactly the G2 combination of probabilities and payoffs. Savage rewrote all four gambles that way. Table 1.1 summarizes the result of this rewriting, and also brings out some similarities among the gambles that had not previously been apparent.

Here is how Savage continues with his own report of the thought experiment, after the gambles had been rewritten:

> If one of the tickets numbered from 12 through 100 is drawn, it will not matter, in either situation, which gamble I choose. I therefore

focus on the possibility that one of the tickets numbered from 1 through 11 will be drawn, in which case situations A1 and A2 are exactly parallel. The subsidiary decision depends in both situations on whether I would sell an outright gift of $500,000 for a 10-to-1 chance to win $2,500,000—a conclusion that I think has a claim to universality, or objectivity. Finally, consulting my purely personal taste, I find that I would prefer the gift of $500,000 and, accordingly, that I prefer Gamble 1 to Gamble 2 and (contrary to my initial reaction) Gamble 3 to Gamble 4.[15]

The crucial move in Savage's reasoning is that since G1 and G2 have the same consequences in the cases where one of the lottery tickets numbered 12–100 is drawn, we should decide between G1 and G2 solely on the basis of the consequences of one of the lottery tickets 1–11 being drawn. Similarly for our choice between G3 and G4.

Immediately before redescribing the four gambles, Savage motivated that move with the remark: "I have since accepted the following way of looking at the two situations, which amounts to a repeated use of the sure-thing principle."

The sure-thing principle, one element of Savage's recommended set of decision-making principles, is closely related to Principle P. Here are the two principles, for comparison:

> *Sure-thing principle:* If someone should not prefer f to g, either knowing that the event B obtained, or knowing that the event not-B obtained, then he should not prefer f to g. Moreover (provided that he does not regard B as virtually impossible), if he should definitely prefer g to f, knowing that B obtained, and, if he should not prefer f to g, knowing that B did not obtain, then he definitely should prefer g to f.[16]
>
> *Principle P:* If someone should prefer having performed act g to having performed act f, either knowing that the event B obtained or knowing that the event not-B obtained, then the person should prefer g to f in fact (that is, before learning whether B or not-B obtains).

Savage uses the form of words "would prefer" rather than the form of words "should prefer." As I said earlier, it is not clear whether he meant STP to be purely prescriptive—in which case it would have been better to write "should prefer"—or whether he meant it to be at least in part descriptive. I will assume he meant it only prescriptively. I will rewrite his "would"s as "should"s.

The second clause of STP (the part following "Moreover") resembles Principle P in that it tells us how to extract what preferences a person should have *in fact* from information about what preferences the person should have if he were in possession of the information whether or not an event B obtains. The difference between Principle P and the second part of STP is that Principle P is a form of "strong dominance principle," whereas the second half of STP is a form of "weak dominance principle." Principle P says, in effect, that if one choice "dominates" another (should be the preferred choice) in every possible circumstance, then that dominant choice should be the agent's actual preference. The second clause of STP says, in effect, that if one choice should not be dispreferred to another in any possible circumstance, and what is more, in one possible circumstance the first choice positively should be preferred to the other choice, then that ("weakly dominant") choice should be preferred by the agent in fact. In STP and Principle P, the choices are labeled schematically f and g, and the possible circumstances are labeled "B obtains" and either "not-B obtains" or "B does not obtain."

But it is not the second, "dominance-principle" half of STP that Savage marshals to argue that the lottery outcomes from "ticket 12 wins" through "ticket 100 wins" can be ignored in assessing what choices to make in his rewritten form of the Allais Problem. What matters is the first clause of STP—what we may as well call the "nonpreference clause." Putting "should" for "would" throughout, the nonpreference clause says: If the person should not prefer f to g, either knowing that the event B obtained, or knowing that the event not-B obtained, then in fact he should not prefer f to g. Principle P contains no parallel nonpreference clause. So, although Principle P is simpler and useful for making the points I have made thus far, it will not help us understand Savage's reasoning in connection with his "rewritten" Allais Problem. Here is how that reasoning goes, or rather, here is how it seems to go (Savage is very terse here).

Consider the tickets 12–100 as tickets in a separate "sublottery." This sublottery may or may not be held. If a ticket from 12 to 100 is drawn in the actual lottery, we will consider the sublottery to have been held. Otherwise, we will consider it not to have been held. Now focus just on the sublottery. Let the events B and not-B be "Ticket 12 is drawn" and

"Ticket 12 is not drawn." Whichever event occurs, I would win $500,000 if I accept gamble G1, and I would win $500,000 if I accept gamble G2. So, whichever event occurs, I should not prefer G1 to G2, and I should not prefer G2 to G1. By two applications of the first, nonpreference clause of STP, I should not prefer G1 to G2 in fact, and I should not prefer G2 to G1 in fact. This reasoning can be repeated when "Ticket 13 is drawn" is *B* and "Ticket 13 is not drawn" is not-*B*. The reasoning can be repeated for each of the tickets 12 to 100. A similar argument can be given when G3 and G4 are being compared. Presumably, this is what Savage means by "a repeated use" of the sure-thing principle.

When Savage initially confronted the Allais Gamble, his thinking must have gone along the lines I earlier ascribed to "most people" (with the suggestion that you, the reader, probably thought along those lines). Savage preferred G1 to G2 because he preferred the absolute certainty of getting a large payoff (G1) to a very small chance of getting nothing, even taken together with a fairly high probability of a very large payoff (G2). And he preferred G4 to G3 because he was not willing to give up one chance in ten of winning $2,500,000 (G4) in order to have a negligibly higher chance of winning $500,000 (G3). It is very easy to understand the choice of G4 over G3. G4 strikes most of us, and no doubt struck Savage, as clearly the "better bet." But we can easily imagine someone having an epistemic policy that dictates Savage's original pattern of choices between G1 and G2 as well. Although the person is willing to take risks in many situations, when he has a choice between getting a substantial prize for sure and taking an uncertain gamble with a larger prize, he takes the certain prize. Call this the "certainty policy." We can also easily imagine someone else, by nature less attracted to a risk-free life, who doesn't adopt the certainty policy. When confronting the Allais Gamble, this second person simply maximizes expected utility.

When Savage saw that his initial response to the Allais Problem was inconsistent with expected utility maximization, he did not conclude that there were two equally "valid," though sometimes conflicting, principles of practical inference: "maximize expected utility" and the "certainty policy." Accepting this result would be tantamount to accepting defeat for his project, since then the requirement to maximize expected utility would no longer have the status usually attributed to principles of logic. Instead, Savage argued that the formulation of the bets had misled him. His thinking seems to have gone as follows.

In a decision problem, the "elements of structure" that ought to matter to a rational agent are: (1) a set of possible states of the world; (2) a set of possible actions; and (3) for each possible action, a set consisting of the consequences of that action in each possible state of the world. An agent will have preferences among the consequences, and these preferences ultimately will dictate preferences among the possible actions. What matters for my purposes here is that by Savage's lights, the proper use of the "elements of structure" is to compare possible actions by comparing the consequences of those actions, possible state of the world by possible state of the world.

But a person who adopts the "certainty policy" violates this last requirement. The certainty policy demands that one have, and apply, the knowledge that a given possible action has a given consequence (e.g., some given dollar amount won) in all possible states of the world. This goes beyond merely knowing, possible state of the world by possible state of the world, that the possible action has the given consequence in that possible state of the world. (One must add in the "global" or "extremal" knowledge that these are all the possible states of the world there are.)[17]

So Savage redescribed the four gambles in a way that clearly brought out the elements of structure he believed to matter. The tabular, lottery-ticket format makes it easy to identify the set of possible states of the world (possible states are determined by which lottery ticket is drawn), a set of possible actions for each of the two "situations" (in situation A1, the set "take gamble G1" and "take gamble G2"; in situation A2, the set "take gamble G3," and "take gamble G4"), and a set consisting of the consequence of each action in each possible state of the world ("win so-and-so much money").

This reformulation made it easy to see which choices the sure-thing principle would dictate, since the STP makes use of, and only of, the "elements of structure" that have now been laid bare. But the relevance, if any, of the "certainty principle" has been obscured. The needed information—that one gamble in situation A1 is a risk-free winner—can be read off from the table. But before taking a look at such things, Savage uses the STP to simplify the decision problem, lopping off the right-hand side of the table. Once that surgery has been performed, the "global" information that one bet is a winner in all possible states of the world is gone. It cannot be discerned from the left-hand side of the table alone. So if one first simplifies and then evaluates the bets intuitively, as

Savage does, the nasty "certainty principle" no longer has any clout. Evidently, when Savage asks himself "how he would react if he noticed himself violating" the rule of expected utility maximization, he discovers that he would redescribe the situation until the urge goes away.

But—why isn't Savage's argument circular? He is aiming to defend a set of principles that, taken together, constitute a form of subjective expected utility theory. When confronted with a case in which it seems rational—rationally permissible, even if not rationally required—to make decisions in a way that violates SEUT, he debunks this criticism by means of an argument that relies, in part, on one of the very principles he wants to defend from attack.

This is not really a circular argument. The fairest interpretation of Savage's meaning is this: Once the four bets are redescribed in terms that lay bare the important elements of structure—the possible states of the world, the possible actions, the consequences—one *intuits* that one need not pay any attention to possible states of the world where the actions being compared have exactly the same consequences. This is an analysis that would be dictated by the sure-thing principle if it were applied; but it is unnecessary to first affirm STP as a theoretician, and then, circularly, apply it in order to defend one's theory from an objection. One's intuitions are clear once the lottery has been suitably redescribed, Savage might say. A rigorous spelling-out of the content of those intuitions would make use of the sure-thing principle. But it is the intuitions themselves—in particular, the intution that one may ignore the implications of one's choices if tickets 12–100 happen to be drawn—that are carrying the weight of debunking the criticism. Understood in this way, there is no circularity in the ordinary sense of the term.

There are other objections to Savage's procedure. One possible objection, related to but not identical with a charge of circularity, is that Savage's intuitions in this matter have reduced authority because of the experimenter effect. In case the idea of "the experimenter effect" is unfamiliar to the reader, here is a brief summary.

A linguist constructing a grammar, for example a transformational grammar of some natural language, cannot simply ask a native speaker what rules she has internalized, since she only has tacit knowledge of these rules. In order to determine what the rules are, the linguist must elicit well-formedness judgments from a native speaker. The native speaker could be the linguist herself.

But then the linguist's reasoning can be challenged by pointing out that the grammaticality intuitions of a native speaker who is also a linguist are a comparatively unreliable indicator of her internalized grammatical rules, since she is subject to an experimenter effect. It has been shown that linguists tend to hear as grammatical those sentences predicted to be grammatical by the linguistic theories they favor.

The experimenter effect has been studied in a number of experiments. Here is one illustration.

Consider the three sentences:

(a) We received plans to kill Bill.
(b) We received plans to kill each other.
(c) We received plans to kill me.

W. Labov reports that in a study of 19 subjects who were not familiar with the theoretical issues involved in analyzing these sentences, using a four-point scale of acceptability, only one subject marked (b) as worse than (a) and (c). Nine found (a) and (b) the same and (c) worse, while seven found all three the same. In another study of 20 subjects, none thought (b) was worse than (c). Introspecting, Noam Chomsky found (b) unacceptable, (c) better. Chomsky's theory at the time dictated this, although it would not have been a crucial objection had his thought experiment come out differently. A simple adjustment would have sufficed. But no adjustment was needed. Experiment confirmed theory, even though it appears Chomsky could not have obtained that experimental result with almost any native speaker other than himself as a source of grammaticality data.[18]

The proponent of a theory about the grammar of her language is much more likely to confirm this theory in a thought experiment than other people are. Sometimes the term "experimenter effect" is used more broadly, to include the tendency of psychologists to observationally confirm their own theories. I am not aware of any tests for the experimenter effect in decision psychology, though it should be straightforward to design such a test. In particular, I am not aware of any tests aimed at determining whether a proponent of a given "normative" decision theory tends to "intuit" as rational the set of choices her theory would dictate, even if she tries to make an "objective and unbiased" intuitive judgment. Nevertheless, it is hard not to think of Savage's intuitions about how, in the end, one should analyze the Allais-Problem set of choices as very similar to Chomsky's grammaticality intuitions as reported by Labov.

A third objection, and, to my mind, a conclusive one, is that Savage has not laid bare all of the structure he ought to have laid bare. There is another layer of structure yet to be revealed, and once we reveal that layer, Savage's argument will look both more complicated and less compelling.

Savage's Argument as a Quasi-Constructive Dilemma

Jack and Casey meet again, and once again Casey shows Jack a philosophical puzzle. This time it is the Allais Problem, with the four gambles described as follows (imagine that Casey has the following text typed on a card).

First consider a hypothetical situation, A1, in which you are offered a choice between two gambles, G1 and G2, and decide which gamble you would accept; second, consider a hypothetical situation, A2, in which you are offered a choice between two gambles, G3 and G4, and decide which gamble you would accept.

This is situation A1:

Choose between:
>   G1:   Win $500,000 with probability 1.
and:
>   G2:   Win $2,500,000 with probability 0.10;
>   win $500,000 with probability 0.89; and
>   remain at the status quo with probability 0.01.

This is situation A2:

Choose between:
>   G3:   Win $500,000 with probability 0.11;
>   remain at the status quo with probability 0.89.
and:
>   G4:   Win $2,500,000 with probability 0.10;
>   remain at the status quo with probability 0.90.

Jack makes Savage's original set of choices and thus chooses G1 from the first pair of gambles and chooses G4 from the second pair. He explains these choices in this way: "I prefer G1 to G2 because G1 gives me a large fortune outright, whereas what G2 gives me is a chance to win a very large fortune, and I don't find this adequate compensation for the small risk of being left at status quo. I prefer G4 to G3, because they give me nearly the same chance of winning something, so the one with the much larger prize seems preferable." I will refer to these reasons as "Jack's original reasons."

Casey tells Jack that his pair of choices is not rational. He tries to convince him that he (Jack) ought to make different choices. Casey begins by suggesting that Jack represent the choices between G1 and G2,

TABLE 1.2.   Casey's lottery-style table.

	Proffered gambles	Lottery ticket number		
		I	2–11	12–100
Situation A1	G1	5	5	5
	G2	0	25	5
Situation A2	G3	5	5	0
	G4	0	25	0
		(payoffs in 100,000 dollars)		

and between G3 and G4, as choices between bets on a lottery. This, he says, will reveal the "real underlying structure" of the decision problem. Casey shows Jack another printed card (table 1.2), this one displaying the table of prizes Savage introduced for his own edification.

Jack agrees that the four gambles are "represented accurately" in table 1.2. With that established, Casey guides Jack in analyzing the table by setting out the following argument, all done up with numbered steps. The argument is a QCD, as is Savage's, though in Savage's presentation the QCD form does not stand out as clearly as it does in Casey's presentation (Casey's directions for reading the table are included at the points where he gave them).

Suppose you play one of the four gambles. Then:

1. Either the ticket that is chosen belongs to the set of results R_{1-11}, or the ticket that is chosen belongs to the set of results R_{12-100}.

2. Suppose the ticket that is chosen belongs to the set of results R_{12-100}. (Stage direction: "Look at the last column.")

3. Since G1 and G2 have the same payoff, $500,000, for the results in the set R_{12-100} and G3 and G4 have the same payoff, $0, for the results in the set R_{12-100}, if the ticket that is chosen belongs to the set of results R_{12-100}, and if I were to choose G2, I would get the same payoff, $500,000, as I would get from choosing G1. Similarly, if I were to choose G3, I would get the same payoff, $0, as I would get from choosing G4.

4. So in this case (one of the tickets 12–100 has been drawn), there is no reason to choose G1 over G2 (or vice versa), and

there is no reason to choose G4 over G3 (or vice versa). Preferring G1 to G2 (or vice versa) is groundless, as is preferring G4 to G3 (or vice versa).

5. Suppose the ticket that is chosen belongs to the set of results R_{1-11}. (stage direction: "look at the first two columns.")

6. Since G1 and G3 have exactly the same payoffs for the results in the set R_{1-11}, as do G2 and G4, if the ticket that is chosen belongs to the set of results R_{1-11}, and if I were to choose G3 over G4, I would get exactly what I would get from choosing G1 over G2. Similarly, choosing G4 over G3 would give me exactly what I would get by choosing G2 over G1.

7. So in this case (one of the tickets 1–11 is chosen), either a choice of G1 over G2 gives me what I disprefer, or else a choice of G4 over G3 gives me what I disprefer, according to what my preferences are like.

8. Therefore, the set of choices G1 over G2 and G4 over G3 is counterpreferential at worst, and groundless at best. Thus it is not rational to so choose.

When Jack is presented with this argument, he is conflicted. Since he can't see anything wrong with it, he is inclined to think that he ought to reverse one of his choices. But, despite the argument's attractions, he is not completely convinced that he ought to do so, since the reasons he had for his original choices still seem good to him. Although Casey's argument provides Jack with reasons for thinking that only certain choices are rationally acceptable, it does not seem to Jack to play the additional role of explaining what is wrong with the reasons he had for his initial pair of choices.

Casey thinks the argument does play this role, since he thinks it shows the incoherence of Jack's choices when they are rephrased in terms of the "real underlying structure" of the decision situation. But Jack is not convinced. When Jack thinks the situation through again, he feels slightly more uncomfortable with Casey's argument than with his own original reasons for his original choices. His own reasons are completely clear to him, whereas Casey's argument has a bit of the feel of a sleight of hand.[19] Thus Jack has misgivings about Casey's argument, although at the same time he finds it hard to ignore and, in particular, he finds Casey's account of the underlying structure of the decision situation intuitively compelling.

Here is my diagnosis of Jack's puzzlement. Jack is uncomfortable with Casey's argument because he is implicitly aware that it is fallacious, although he is unable to make the fallacy explicit. The fallacy involves equivocating, sliding tacitly from one argument to another. The way Casey presents his argument makes this equivocation hard to catch. Casey has broken the argument into "logical modules," short stretches of reasoning, and has encouraged Jack to evaluate each module separately. The way Jack understands each sentence is influenced by the way he understands the other sentences in the module in which the sentence occurs. Jack's understanding of a sentence, his logical parsing of it, shifts from one module to another. These switches in logical parsing of a given sentence from one module to another are hard for Jack to catch and articulate, but he "feels" that there is something unconvincing about the resulting reasoning.

The first logical module consists of the main premise (1). The second module consists of the first subargument, sentences (2), (3), and (4). The third module consists of the second subargument, sentences (5), (6), and (7). The fourth logical module consists of the inference that ties together the initial premise and the conclusions of the two subarguments: lines (1), (4), (7), and (8). Since breaking up the original argument in this way leads Jack to consider each module separately, it diminishes the extent to which the way Jack understands sentences in one module influences the way he understands sentences in another module, and it makes it harder for Jack to notice if he understands the same sentence differently when it occurs in different modules. We must work through this process in detail to see how Jack's modular understanding of the argument leads him to equivocate.

Picking Apart a QCD

Casey began his argument by presenting a table designed to represent the outcomes of each action in the various possible states of the world when these possible states of the world are grouped in a certain way (table 1.3). Casey expected Jack to see that premise (1)

(1) Either the ticket that is chosen belongs to the set of results R_{1-11}, or the ticket that is chosen belongs to the set of results R_{12-100}

is merely a description of a feature made prominent in the setup of the table: that the possible results of the lottery can be divided into two mutually exclusive, jointly exhaustive sets. Jack needs a little background knowledge of lotteries; he needs to know that only one ticket will win, and he needs to know that some ticket will win—that is, if for some reason the lottery is not held, all bets are off. Both Casey and Jack have this background knowledge, so the "lottery" formulation of the "possibilities" involved in the Allais Problem makes good sense to them.

Now, Casey's (and Savage's) reason for describing the four gambles as bets on the outcome of a lottery is to make vivid one of the basic structural features of a decision problem, at least according to Savage (and Casey). A decision problem requires the decision-maker to evaluate the consequences of actions in various possible states of the world. But there is more than one way to understand these alternative "possibilities."

In this case, what is important for Jack's purposes is that he does not know what the result of the lottery is. That is the way the lottery formulation of the decision-making situation captures the idea of uncertainty. Usually when one bets on a lottery, one does not know the result because the lottery has not yet been played. But that is not essential. Jack's

TABLE 1.3.   Casey's lottery-style table, again.

		Lottery ticket number		
		I	2–11	12–100
Situation A1	G1	5	5	5
	G2	0	25	5
Situation A2	G3	5	5	0
	G4	0	25	0
		(payoffs in 100,000 dollars)		

uncertainty would be captured equally well if the lottery had already been played but Jack did not know the result. The set of "possibilities" relevant to Jack's decision-making would be the same whether or not the lottery had been played. The possibilities are epistemic; they are determined by the state of Jack's knowledge.[20]

Thus, before Jack knows the result of the lottery, the result that ticket 1 is chosen is a "possibility" for Jack, the result that ticket 2 is chosen is a possibility for Jack, and so on for each of the 100 possible results of the lottery. But once Jack knows what this result is, there is only one epistemically possible lottery result for Jack. So what is epistemically possible for Jack changes as he acquires new information.[21]

Once Casey has obtained Jack's agreement that premise (1) must be true in light of the way the lottery is designed, he tries to convince Jack to accept the first of two subarguments. To begin this subargument, Jack is asked to "suppose" the second disjunct of (1). That supposition occurs as sentence (2) of Casey's argument taken as a whole:

(2) Suppose the ticket that is chosen belongs to the set of results R_{12-100}.

How does Jack understand sentence (2)? If the argument taken as a whole is to be valid, then in "supposing" (2), Jack must be supposing that one of the disjuncts of (1) is true. So he ought to understand this disjunct of (1) when it occurs as (2) the same way he understands it when it occurs as a disjunct of (1). This is a point of logic. Jack must understand (2) in this way in order for Casey's argument to be valid. But what reason is there to believe that Jack's understanding of the language of Casey's argument is influenced by an inclination to make Casey's argument valid? Since I will want to posit similar influences again and again in what follows, we should pause to consider how plausible such posits are.

My argument rests on a Gricean principle, by which I mean a principle in the spirit of P. Grice's conception of "cooperation" among conversants. This is the principle:

Principle G: In a conversation between two partners, each partner interprets the words of the other in such a way as to make those words most plausible by the standards the interpreter believes the other partner obeys, and the interpreter expects the other partner to do the same in her role as interpreter. In particular, when partner A gives an argument, partner B interprets that argument so that it is an argument that B judges that A would consider valid, and partner B expects partner A to interpret her (B's) arguments similarly.

In most circumstances, Principle G can be replaced by the simpler Principle G*:

> Principle G*: In a conversation between two partners, each partner interprets the words of the other in such a way as to make those words most plausible, and expects the other to do the same. In particular, when one partner gives an argument, the other interprets that argument so as to make it valid (as she judges).

The simpler principle usually is correct, because conversational partners usually follow almost exactly the same rules of inference, and expect this of each other. Conversations rarely happen "across conceptual frameworks," where Principle G* might be violated even though Principle G still holds. Hereafter, I will use the simpler Principle G*.

If conversational practice did not normally obey Principle G (or what usually amounts to the same thing, Principle G*), the practice of conversation would be cumbersome in the best case and impossible in the worst case. I do not know how to prove this claim. It seems obvious to me. Consider the following (actual) example of what happens when Principle G* is violated.[22]

In 1992, during the flight of the Magellan space probe, NASA collected data about the planet Venus. They then made a video animation of a flight around Venus relatively close to its surface. This animation makes Venus look as if it has a dramatic landscape made up of steep canyons and soaring mountains. A typical viewer of this video had no prior information about the surface of Venus, and needed to make some decision (tacitly) about how to interpret what she was seeing. In particular, a typical viewer of the video needed to apply scales, and ratios of scales. For instance, she needed to decide on a ratio between vertical and horizontal scale. Scales, and such things as ratios of scales, are principles of inference, although it is visual, nonverbal, inference.

Obeying Principle G*, viewers of the video assumed the NASA officials who had made it intended to represent ratios of vertical to horizontal dimensions on the surface of Venus by closely corresponding ratios (or apparent ratios) in the video image. No doubt the NASA officials expected this interpretation. Viewers of the video came away believing the surface of Venus to be craggy and dramatic—the intended result.

But in fact, NASA increased the vertical scale 22.5 times relative to the horizontal scale. The volcanoes that are so dramatic in the video have heights of up to 5 kilometers and widths of several hundred kilometers, so that the mean slopes are no more than 3 degrees. Not very dramatic at all.

Viewers who learned these facts were not, and are not, happy about it. They tend to mistrust similar videos produced by NASA, suspecting that they should not draw the "usual" visual inferences. But they do not know what visual inferences they should draw instead. Certainly that is my own reaction. The result is that Principle G⋆ (and Principle G) does not apply to my "conversations" with NASA about conditions on the surface of planets, moons, and so forth. I am dependent on precisely such representational devices as video animations, because it would do me no good for NASA scientists to send me quantities of raw data. At best, I might extract a few scattered samples of information about surface features, but nothing even close to the rich knowledge, the "continuous picture," I could get from an animation I trusted.

The final result is that I cannot "converse" with NASA about these matters. There is nothing special about this case. By picking an example where Principle G⋆ breaks down for visual inference, as opposed to verbal inference, the damage done to the possibility of conversation is perhaps more striking, because when expectations about rules of visual inference are undermined, the loss in information, relative to what one might have obtained, is enormous. So the point is very striking in such a case, as I intended. But there would be a similar, if less pronounced, effect if the rule of inference that had been undermined were verbal.

Now just imagine a widespread breakdown of Principle G⋆, exactly like the breakdown that occurs when one learns about NASA's video "faking." Conversation often would lose its point, since the chief point, or an important subsidiary point, of almost all conversation is the sharing of information. So we can say that the fact that people normally obey Principle G⋆ (or, in general, Principle G) is a requirement for conversation to occur at all. Part of what is involved in learning to converse is learning to honor Principle G⋆. Breakdowns of this practice can only occur rarely, and with serious consequences for communication when they do occur.[23]

Jack, therefore, obeys Principle G⋆ in his conversation with Casey. So the fact that in order for Casey's argument to be valid, sentence (2) must be understood exactly the way it is understood when it occurs as a disjunct of (1) puts pressure on Jack to so understand (2). But there is also pressure on Jack to understand (2) in a different way. This pressure comes from the fact that (2) occurs as an element of another logical module. In addition to being a disjunct of the main premise of Casey's argument taken as a whole, (2) is a premise of the first subargument. We must see why this matters.

Recall that since Jack is faced with the task of making a decision where the facts (the lottery outcome) are uncertain, the "possibilities" he envisages are epistemic. As a result, when Jack is asked to "suppose" that the ticket that is chosen belongs to the set of results R_{12-100}, it is very natural for him to understand this as requiring him to imagine that he has come to know that the ticket that is chosen belongs to the set of results R_{12-100}. This is not the way one ordinarily intends a "supposition" that one intends to discharge as the reasoning proceeds. One intends that the supposition be "imagined true," so that one can see what follows under the assumption that things are that way. In order to imagine that a proposition is true, one need not imagine that, in addition, one knows the proposition. But in the context of practical reasoning under uncertainty, this distinction is easily blurred. Jack would be inclined to understand the request "Suppose the ticket that is chosen belongs to the set of results 12–100" as a request to narrow down the envisaged epistemic possibilities so that the only epistemic possibilities are "ticket 12 is chosen," "ticket 13 is chosen," . . . , "ticket 100 is chosen" (and some logical combinations of these; e.g., "either ticket 33 is chosen or ticket 98 is chosen"). Narrowing the epistemic possibilities in this way is equivalent to pretending that one has obtained the information that a ticket in the set 12–100 has in fact been chosen, or will be chosen.

To keep straight which way of understanding (2) we are talking about at a given moment, let us use the labels "(2 K)" and "(2 not-K)" for two different ways Jack might understand what (2) asks him to imagine obtains:

(2 K) It is true that the ticket that is chosen belongs to the set of results R_{12-100}, and I know this.

and:

(2 not-K) It is true that the ticket that is chosen belongs to the set of results R_{12-100}, although I do not know this.

Corresponding to (2 K) and (2 not-K) are two understandings of (1):

> (1 K) It is true that the ticket that is chosen belongs to the set of results R_{I-II}, and I know this, or it is true that the ticket that is chosen belongs to the set of results R_{12-100}, and I know this.
>
> and:
>
> (1 not-K) It is true that the ticket that is chosen belongs to the set of results R_{I-II}, although I do not know this, or it is true that the ticket that is chosen belongs to the set of results R_{12-100}, although I do not know this.

Jack knows he is making his decision before the lottery is played. This will lead him to understand (1) as (1 not-K). In order for (2) to be a disjunct of (1 not-K), it must be understood as (2 not-K). And in order for Jack to understand Casey's argument in such a way that it is valid, (2) must be a disjunct of (1). The "Gricean" Principle G* inclines Jack to interpret Casey's words so as to make his argument valid. Therefore, there is pressure on Jack to understand (2) as (2 not-K).

As I have shown, however, since (2) also occurs in a second logical module, steps (2), (3), and (4) of Casey's argument, where it functions as a supposition to be discharged, there is pressure on Jack to understand (2) as (2 K), since it is natural for Jack to interpret the instruction to "suppose" (2) as meaning that he should suppose he has *learned* that (2) is the case.

Does the fact that (2) is an element of the logical module (2), (3), (4) influence Jack's understanding of (2) for any reason other than this? We need to explore that issue. Here once again is the module (2), (3), (4):

2. Suppose the ticket that is chosen belongs to the set of results R_{12-100}. (Stage direction: "look at the last column.")

3. Since G1 and G2 have the same payoff, $500,000, for the results in the set R_{12-100} and G3 and G4 have the same payoff, $0, for the results in the set R_{12-100}, if the ticket that is chosen belongs to the set of results R_{12-100}, and if I were to choose G2, I would get the same payoff, $500,000, as I would get from choosing G1. Similarly, if I were to choose G3, I would get the same payoff, $0, as I would get from choosing G4.

4. So in this case (one of the tickets 12–100 has been drawn), there is no reason to choose G1 over G2 (or vice versa), and there is no reason to choose G4 over G3 (or vice versa).

Preferring G1 to G2 (or vice versa) is groundless, as is preferring G4 to G3 (or vice versa).

In order to understand how the rest of the module affects the way
Jack understands (2), we first have to see how Jack understands (4).
Sentence (4) occurs both in the second module of the argument, the one
I am now considering, and the module of the argument that leads Jack
from (1), and the conclusions of the subarguments, (4) and (7), to (8), the
conclusion of the argument as a whole. Here is that module separated
out from the rest of the argument:

1. Either the ticket that is chosen belongs to the set of results R_{1-11},
   or the ticket that is chosen belongs to the set of results R_{12-100}.

4. So in this case (one of the tickets 12–100 has been drawn),
   there is no reason to choose G1 over G2 (or vice versa), and
   there is no reason to choose G4 over G3 (or vice versa).
   Preferring G1 to G2 (or vice versa) is groundless, as is preferring G4 to G3 (or vice versa).

7. So in this case (one of the tickets 1–11 is chosen) either a
   choice of G1 over G2 gives me what I disprefer, or else a
   choice of G4 over G3 gives me what I disprefer, according to
   what my preferences are like.

8. Therefore, the set of choices G1 over G2 and G4 over G3 is
   counterpreferential at worst, and groundless at best. Thus it is
   not rational to so choose.

Jack is aware that the point of Casey's argument is to show him that
his original set of choices was irrational, and thereby to get him to make
different choices. Thus, since (8) is the conclusion of the whole argument, it is likely that Jack will understand (8) as making that point. As
such, Jack is likely to understand (8) as a criticism of his set of choices,
given the epistemic position he is in at the time he makes those choices. I
will call a criticism of Jack's choices from the perspective of the epistemic
position Jack is in when he makes those choices a criticism of the *rationality* of Jack's decision. This should be distinguished from another
type of criticism of the *quality of* Jack's decision: a criticism of Jack's
decision in light of information *that Jack receives about the world after the
time at which he makes his decision.* I will call a criticism of this kind a
backtracking criticism of Jack's decision. Given what Jack understands the

point of Casey's argument to be, Jack will be inclined to understand (8) as a criticism of the rationality of his decision rather than as a back-tracking criticism of his decision. So Jack will be inclined to understand (8) as (8R) rather than as (8B):

> (8R) From the point of view of the rationality of these choices, the pair of choices, G1 over G2, and G4 over G3, is either groundless or counterpreferential, and therefore it is not rational to make both of them.
>
> (8B) From the point of view of what I will, eventually, learn, the set of choices G1 over G2, and G4 over G3, is either groundless or counter-preferential, and therefore it is not rational to make both of them.

The distinction between a criticism of the rationality of a decision and a backtracking criticism of that decision will play an important role in what follows. To be sure that the distinction is clear, here are two cases where decisions are criticized as pointless, the first of which is a criticism of the rationality of the decision and the second a backtracking criticism of the decision.

If I take an umbrella when I leave the house, even though I am aware that there is virtually no chance of rain, someone can call my tak-ing the umbrella pointless, since, given the information I had at the time I decided whether or not to take the umbrella, it was unreasonable for me to think I would need it. This judgment of pointlessness is a criticism of the rationality of my decision.

If I take an umbrella when I leave the house because I have good reason to believe that it is going to rain, but I observe that it does not rain in the course of my trip out of the house, someone might call my decision to take an umbrella pointless on the grounds that, as I eventually learn, I would not have gotten wet even if I had not taken an umbrella. That is a backtracking criticism of my decision. I could defend myself against the "backtracking" judgment of pointlessness if it was meant as a criticism of the rationality of my decision on the grounds that it was not fair—my decision wasn't pointless, given the epistemic position I was in when I made it, though from the point of view of my later epistemic position, I can see that it was unnecessary to take an umbrella.

The feature that makes a criticism backtracking is that it is made from the point of view of an epistemic state of the agent after the time at which she actually makes the decision. Usually this is an epistemic state in which the agent is better informed. We do make criticisms of this kind, as when someone says "I just read the sports page. I should have bet on Donald Duck"[24] or "Oops! Look at this. I made a bad choice—I should have bet on Donald Duck." If the horse on which the agent placed her bet was—before the race—as likely a winner as Donald Duck, this is only a self-criticism of her decision in a backtracking sense, though in its way it is a perfectly legitimate kind of criticism. What is essential, though, is that backtracking criticisms not be mistaken for criticisms of the rationality of a choice.

Here is an important point about my definition of a backtracking criticism: Like a criticism of the rationality of a decision, a backtracking criticism is a criticism made from the point of view of an epistemic state of the agent. In the case of a backtracking criticism, the epistemic state is one the agent is in at some time after she makes her choice, when she has additional information. Usually she is "better informed," in the sense that when in her later epistemic state she has less uncertainty about the outcome of the choice in question. The concept of a backtracking criticism must be distinguished from another, related, concept: what we might call a judgment of objective correctness. The agent who decides to take the umbrella not only learns that no rain falls on her; in fact, no rain does fall on her. Taking an umbrella turned out to be objectively unnecessary. Even if she somehow never noticed that no rain fell on her, it would remain true that none did. Someone could criticize her for "needlessly taking an umbrella" (a judgment of objective correctness) in addition to criticizing her for "taking an umbrella, needlessly, as she learned" (a backtracking criticism in my sense). Often it is difficult to tell whether someone criticizing a given decision in a "backward-looking way" is giving a backtracking criticism in my sense, or is making a judgment of the objective correctness of the choice.

Let us pick up the thread where we left it. Since Casey presents his argument to Jack in order to encourage Jack to revise his choices before Jack knows the result of the lottery, the argument is offered by Casey, and likely to be understood by Jack, as a criticism of the rationality of Jack's original decision. Thus Jack will be inclined to understand (8) as (8R). But Jack will see that (4) is a crucial premise in the inference to (8R). Like (8), sentence (4) has a "rationality criticism" interpretation and a "backtracking criticism" interpretation:

(4R) From the point of view of the rationality of these choices, there is no reason to choose G1 over G2, or G4 over G3, so in this sense both of these choices are groundless.

and:

(4B) From the point of view of what I will, eventually, learn, there is no reason to choose G1 over G2, or G4 over G3, so in this sense, both of these choices are groundless.

It is easy to see that only (4R) supports an inference to (8) understood as (8R), whereas (4B) does not support that inference. The fact that a decision is irrational in a backtracking sense does not imply that it is irrational relative to the epistemic state of the decision-maker at the time that he made his decision.[25] So another application of the Gricean Principle G$\star$ gives Jack a reason to understand (4) as (4R). Thus there is pressure on Jack, due to his inclination to validate Casey's argument taken as a whole, to understand (4) as (4R) rather than as (4B). How does this affect Jack's understanding of (2)?

Yet another application of the Gricean principle leads Jack to try to interpret the language of the logical module (2), (3), (4) in such a way that it becomes a valid subargument (though, as always, with applications of the Gricean principle, Jack may not realize it is operative—remember, my use of the phrase "application of the Gricean principle" must not be taken as implying a conscious or calculated interpretation of what words mean). If Jack understands (4) as (4R), how would he have to understand (2) and (3) in order to make a valid argument out of the argument from (2) and (3) to (4) as a conclusion?

Recall that Jack has two alternative ways to understand (2), corresponding to two different sets of epistemic possibilities, a wider set and a narrower set:

(2 K) It is true that the ticket that is chosen belongs to the set of results R_{12-100}, and I know this.

and:

(2 not-K) It is true that the ticket that is chosen belongs to the set of results R_{12-100}, although I do not know this.

(2 K) rules out, as epistemic possibilities, all of the results 1–11. (2 not-K) does not rule out these results; they remain (epistemically) possible. Suppose Jack understood (2) as (2 not-K). Would the argument "(2 not-K), (3), therefore (4R)" be valid? The argument would look like this:

(2 not-K) It is true that the ticket that is chosen belongs to the set of results R_{12-100}, although I do not know this.

(3) Since G1 and G2 have the same payoff, \$500,000, for the results in the set R_{12-100}, and G3 and G4 have the same payoff, \$0, for the results in the set R_{12-100}, if the ticket that is chosen belongs to the set of results R_{12-100}, if I were to choose G2, I would get the same payoff, \$500,000, as I would get from choosing G1, and if I were to choose G3, I would get the same payoff, \$0, as I would from choosing G4.

(4R) From the point of view of the rationality of these choices, there is no reason to choose G1 over G2, or G4 over G3, so in this sense both of these choices are groundless.

Understood in this way, the subargument is not valid. If Jack assumes that after the lottery is held, he will know that the winning ticket falls into the set 12–100 (because it will and he will find out), although he does not know this at the time he makes his decision, then all he has a right to infer is that when he learns the result of the lottery he will see that his initial choices were "groundless" in a backtracking sense.

So, since Jack understands (4) as (4R)—thereby making a good fit between his understanding of the conclusion of the subargument and his understanding of (8), the conclusion of the argument as a whole—and since Jack is moved by Gricean pressure to interpret the subargument (2), (3), (4) so that it is valid, he must understand (2) as (2 K). As I showed earlier, Jack also has a reason to understand (2) as (2 K)—his inclination to regard the "supposition" involved in step (2) as narrowing the set of epistemic possibilities; or to put it in other words, his inclination to regard the "supposition" involved in step (2) as requiring him to suppose he knows (2).[26]

But remember that (2) is one of the disjuncts of (1), and the understanding of (1) that corresponds to (2 K) is (1 K). When Jack considers (1) by itself, or in the context of the logical module (1), (4), (7), (8), he understands (1) as (1 not-K), and accepts it. If he were understanding (1) as (1 K) in these settings, he would reject it, since he knows perfectly well that he does not know how the lottery will turn out. But when Jack shifts his mental gaze to module (2), (3), (4) he does not, as consistency would demand, understand (2) as (2 not-K); he understands it as (2 K). This enables him to interpret the subargument (2), (3), (4) as valid—while *also*, and equally "tacitly"—understanding (4) as (4R), as a subconclusion pertaining to the rationality of his decision, a subconclusion that in its turn fits neatly into an argument for the bottom-line conclusion (8), understood as (8R).

Or so I suggest. This diagnosis makes sense of Jack's inability to put his finger on what bothers him about Casey's argument. Everywhere he looks, so to speak, what he sees looks all right. And my diagnosis also makes sense of Jack's continuing reluctance to accept Casey's argument. Jack is not aware, or at least is not fully aware, of the crucial shifts in his understanding of some of the language of Casey's argument that enable Casey to pull off his "trick." But, I suggest, he has awareness enough to be balky.

All of these considerations apply equally to the way Jack's understanding of sentence (5) is influenced by its role in the logical module (5), (6), (7); that is, its role in the second subargument. When Jack concentrates on the role played by (5) in the module (5), (6), (7), he will be under pressure to understand these sentences as

> (5 K) The ticket that is chosen belongs to the set of results R_{1-11} and I know this.
>
> (6 K) Since G1 and G3 have exactly the same payoffs for the results in the set R_{1-11} as do G2 and G4, if I know that the ticket that is chosen belongs to the set of results R_{1-11}, then I know that if I were to choose G3 over G4, I would get exactly what I would get from choosing G1 over G2, and, similarly, I know that if I were to choose G4 over G3 I would get exactly what I would get from choosing G2 over G1.
>
> and:
>
> (7 K) I know that: Either a choice of G1 over G2 gives me what I disprefer, or else a choice of G4 over G3 gives me what I disprefer, according to what my preferences are like. Thus it is irrational of me to make both of these choices.

The reasons exactly parallel the reasons I described in the case of the module (2), (3), (4), so I will not repeat them.

But when Jack concentrates on (5) as a disjunct of (1), he understands it as

> (5 not-K), The ticket that is chosen belongs to the set of results R_{1-11}, although I do not know this.

Again, it is plausible that Jack fails to "fully see" himself making this shift, but it is also plausible that he dimly sees himself making it and is unsatisfied with Casey's argument for reasons he cannot articulate.

One reason Jack finds it hard to catch his equivocations is that Casey, like Savage, has assumed that a certain level of structure suffices to frame a decision problem. But there is further structure. Criticism of a decision can be from more than one epistemic point of view. It can be from the point of view of what the agent knows at the time the decision is made, or it can be backtracking. By failing to represent this further structure in his table of lottery outcomes, Casey made it possible for Jack to slide back and forth between epistemic points of view.

Logically Exhaustive Backtrackers

Eventually Jack sees that he has been misled into equivocating. It occurs to him that his unstable understanding of the words Casey used in this argument about which gambles to accept is exactly analogous to the unstable understanding he had of Casey's words when Casey first presented him with the Chimp Argument, once upon a time during another walk through the park.

Here is how Jack explains the parallel with the Chimp Argument:

JACK: You recall, Casey, that when you first told me about the Chimp Argument, you framed the argument in language that was subject to more than one understanding. Really, there were two different arguments, but I was failing to discriminate them from one another. Because I mixed up these two arguments, I failed to notice that on neither interpretation was the Chimp Argument sound. Or rather, I failed to notice this fully and consciously. I did have reservations about the argument that I could not articulate. That is exactly what has happened here.

I had trouble seeing what was going on here because when you set up your argument you did not provide enough information about the epistemic "point of view" from which the reasoning was meant to proceed. I was conflating epistemic points of view, rather than conflating quantifier orders, as I did with the Chimp Argument.

CASEY: You may be right about that. But I can reformulate my argument in a way that makes clear the "epistemic point of view" at each stage, and that rests on a compelling principle of reasoning. Perhaps it is not quite a valid principle in the logician's sense of the term, but it is so compelling we might as well call it "valid" in a looser sense.

Casey then shows Jack a card on which he has written the following.

Principle B (for "backtracking")

Suppose an agent is trying to decide between two possible actions, f and g. Let e_1 be the state of knowledge of this agent at the time she is making her decision. Suppose the agent knows she will receive information that will put her in one or the other of two possible states of knowledge, e_2 or e_3. Assume that e_2 and e_3 exclude each other, and exhaust the possible states of knowledge the agent may be in upon receiving further information—or rather, they exhaust the possible states of knowledge she may be in that would be relevant to her choosing between performing f and performing g.

Clause (1): Assume that if the agent were to be in e_2, she would see that she *should not have chosen f* over *g*; and moreover, if she were to be in e_3, she would see that she *should have chosen g* over *f*. And assume she can see that these things are so even when she is still in e_1. Then, *even when she is still in* e_1, she should choose to perform *g* rather than *f*.

Clause (2): Assume that if the agent were to be in either e_2 or e_3, she would see that she *should have chosen g* over *f*, and assume that she can see that these things are so even when she is still in e_1. Then, *even when she is still in* e_1, she should choose to perform *g* rather than *f*.

CASEY: Now you can see, Jack, that Principle B has two clauses. These clauses recommend that the agent's choices be evaluated from the perspective of information the agent can be sure she will possess—because the information is logically exhaustive. So your objection to backtracking evaluation does not apply. It may be helpful to think of (1) as an "epistemic form" of the weak dominance principle, whereas (2) is an epistemic form of the strong dominance principle. By "epistemic form" I mean to imply that the alternative states of the world invoked by these formulations of dominance principles are states of the agent's knowledge. When clause (1) or clause (2) of Principle B is the rule of inference employed in a piece of practical reasoning, I call the resulting argument a "logically exhaustive backtracker." All such arguments are valid.

As an example of a logically exhaustive backtracker, I will give you an argument that shows you should not make the pair of choices G1 over G2 and G4 over G3 when you consider the Allais Problem in the lottery format (see table 1.4).

TABLE 1.4.   Casey's lottery-style table, one more time.

		Lottery ticket number		
		1	2–11	12–100
Situation A1	G1	5	5	5
	G2	0	25	5
Situation A2	G3	5	5	0
	G4	0	25	0
		(payoffs in 100,000 dollars)		

The argument goes as follows. Let e_1 be the epistemic state you are in now, as you consider which gambles in each pair you should prefer. Let e_2 be the epistemic state you would be in if you learned that a ticket numbered 12–100 had been drawn. Let e_3 be the epistemic state you would be in if you learned a ticket numbered 1–11 had been drawn.

If you were to be in e_2, you would see that you should be indifferent between having chosen G1 or G2, and you would see that you should be indifferent between having chosen G3 or G4. On the other hand, if you were to be in e_3, you would see that you should prefer having chosen G1 over G2 and G3 over G4, or else you should prefer having chosen G2 over G1 and G4 over G3. Certainly you should not prefer having chosen G1 over G2 and G4 over G3. So, by clause (1) of Principle B, you should prefer G1 to G2 and G3 to G4, or else you should prefer G2 to G1 and G4 to G3.

I do not see how you can reject this reasoning without rejecting dominance reasoning in the theory of rational choice. I might add that the Businessman Argument, which you have agreed is persuasive, also follows Principle B, except that clause (2) is operative. The Businessman Argument is an example of strong dominance reasoning.

JACK: I don't like your argument, Casey, and since you are right that your argument follows Principle B, I don't like Principle B. Clause (1) of Principle B obliges me to make separate decisions about what I should prefer to have done in the event that I wind up in e_2 and in the event that I wind up in e_3. But by doing that, I disguise from myself the fact that G1 is a certain, guaranteed, winner. I chose G1 over G2 because I have a "certainty policy." I attach significant positive value to bets (or other possible actions) that are certain, guaranteed, winners. Now, when I imagined myself in epistemic state e_2, I imagined coming to know that a ticket numbered 12–100 had been drawn. If I really did know that—even if I did not know which ticket in the 12–100 range was drawn, *both* G1 *and* G2 would offer a certain win of $500,000. G1 would no longer be special in that respect. But given my actual epistemic state, G1 *is* special, and has a "certainty policy advantage" over G2.

And, when I imagined myself in epistemic state e_3, I was imagining having learned that a ticket numbered 1–11 had been drawn. If I really were in possession of that information, then I would see that G1 was a certain winner, as opposed to G2. But G3 *also* would be a certain winner, as opposed to G4. In all other respects, G3 would stand to G4 exactly as

G1 stood to G2. So if I applied my certainty policy when deciding between G1 and G2, consistency would demand that I apply it when deciding between G3 and G4 as well. That is not how things are in reality, when I have not received any information about the lottery's outcome. In reality, G1 is the only one of the four gambles that enjoys a certainty policy advantage.

Principle B distorts the way my certainty policy applies when I evaluate the four gambles in the Allais Problem. Evidently you do not employ a certainty policy when you evaluate choices, so this defect in Principle B does not bother you. But it bothers me, and it does not help in the slightest that e_2 and e_3 exhaust the possibilities for relevant in- formation I might come to possess.[27]

At this point, it was clear to Jack and Casey that they were at an impasse. Jack placed a great deal of weight on a certainty policy that Casey did not feel moved by. They decided to stop debating the Allais problem for the time being and make an attempt to get to the bottom of their differences over the certainty policy, and other similar policies, if there were any others. So Jack decided to do a little philosophical analysis. He began by telling Casey a story.

JACK: I have been seeing a psychiatrist lately. He has explained to me that I have two related problems. Taken together, they have caused me a lot of anguish. I am unable to reward myself for success and I always punish myself for failure. My psychiatrist suggested that I adopt a policy of acting counter to these two tendencies. When I learn I have succeeded at something important to me, I should work hard at wanting to be re- warded. The best reward for this purpose would be something that provided pure, uncomplicated pleasure—such as lying on a beach in Hawaii. And when I learn I have failed at something important to me, once again I should work hard at wanting to give myself a purely pleasurable experience—such as lying on a beach in Hawaii.

My psychiatrist and I discussed techniques for manipulating one's desires that are effective at least in the short term, especially when the object of desire is a purely pleasurable experience. One technique was this: Make the intended object of desire "special." Pick something which, though pleasurable, is not at all the sort of experience you would ordinarily permit yourself to have. In fact (this should be thought of as part of the policy) do what you can to avoid wanting this special reward, that is, wanting it all things considered, when you have not learned of an important success or failure on your part. I thought this would be easy for me, since as you know, Casey, I do not permit myself very many pure pleasures. I thought lying on a beach in Hawaii was a very good choice, and that is what I settled on. I was eager for an opportunity to implement the policy my psychiatrist recommended.

An opportunity came soon. I had just taken a tough qualifying examination and did not yet know the results. As I waited for the day the results would be announced, I was offered a great price on a vacation package to Hawaii. Luckily, I was also offered the opportunity to pay a five-dollar fee to retain the right to buy the the same vacation package, at the same price, later, after the exam results had been announced.

Now, if it had not been for my new policy, I would have walked away from the deal with just a twinge of regret. As much fun as it would be to lie on a Hawaiian beach, I would have preferred to pass up the chance. By a small margin, I would prefer to stay home and hang out with friends. If I failed the exam, I would be disconsolate, and my friends could console me; if I passed the exam, my friends could help me celebrate, quietly and tastefully and without having too much fun. In fact, these were exactly my desires before learning the results of the exam, which were not announced for several days. At that point, before I actually learned of my success or actually learned of my failure, my new policy did not dictate that I form the all-in desire to go lie on a beach—indeed my policy dictated that I not do so, to preserve the "special" character of Hawaii vacations.

That is why I say it was lucky that I could pay a small fee and buy the vacation package later. After I learned whether I had passed or had failed, my new policy would dictate that I form the desire to go to Hawaii. By paying the small fee I was able to act on that desire, once I formed it, at minimal expense.

Now, the reason I am telling you this story, Casey, is that I believe my decisions were rational. But they were in violation of clause (2) of Principle B. There were two possible future epistemic states for me to consider, knowing I had passed and knowing I had failed. I could see that were I to *enter* either of those states, I would prefer going to Hawaii to not going to Hawaii. Entering one of these epistemic states would be learning of a success or learning of a failure, so the policy my shrink recommended would kick in. It would be fairly easy to "let myself" form the desire for a pure pleasure, especially since I would have an honorable "self-improvement" rationale for so doing. And that is exactly what happened.

But when I was in my initial epistemic state, one in which I had not yet received information about the outcome of the exam, I preferred not to purchase the vacation package, because I preferred not to go to Hawaii. Principle B entails that even before I learned whether I had passed or had failed, I should, rationally, have preferred to buy the vacation package. That would have secured for me the same cheap rates I eventually paid, and saved me the cost of the small fee. But in fact what I did was the rational thing, contrary to Principle B. This shows that Principle B is invalid.

The reason Principle B fails in the circumstances I described is this: Information concerning the results of the exam has a *rational value* for me that goes beyond its value as evidence for what the facts are. When I say the information has a "rational value," I mean the information provides me with a good reason to choose one way rather than another. This contrasts with situations in which receiving information simply *causes* someone's preferences to change, but does not fit into a rational policy the person has. I have described an especially simple example of this phenomenon, an example where merely coming into possession of certain information provides me with a rational basis for acting one way rather than another, but where this is not due to the information serving as evidence for what the world is like. There are other ways in which information can have rational value, but not merely as further evidence for what the facts are. In a moment I will tell you, at the risk of boring you, how this happens in the case of the Allais Problem.

First I want to introduce some helpful terminology. Let us say that when information has rational value for a decision-maker, but this value is not due merely to the evidentiary or probative role the information plays, the information is *ellsbergian for* that decision-maker, and plays an *ellsbergian role* in her decision-making. Now suppose the decision maker has a general policy according to which her decisions are to be made with certain types of information treated as Ellsbergian for her. Let us say that such a policy is an *ellsbergian policy*.

Principle B, in fact "epistemic dominance" or "sure-thing" reasoning in general, ignores the possibility of ellsbergian information, and ignores the possibility of a rational ellsbergian policy. For example, a proponent of clause (1) of Principle B reasons that once I am sure that regardless what information I come to possess—that is, *regardless what the facts prove to be*, I cannot go wrong choosing a certain action X, and it is possible that by choosing X, I will do better than I could do with any other choice, then I should choose X. But this assumes that the only role new information can have in rational decision-making is as evidence for what the facts are. That is not true. In the case I just described of a policy recommended by my shrink, for example, new information plays a role in addition to its role as evidence for what the facts are; it matters to me, rationally, *that I have come to possess it*. And in the case of my certainty policy, new information can matter to me because it alters the *global structure* of my set of epistemic possibilities.

Now let me return to the four gambles in the Allais Problem. What happens is this: When it is certain, or nearly certain, that I will win if I take a particular bet rather than taking some alternative, I strongly prefer the certain win, even if an informal expected utility calculation shows that the certain win offers a lower expected utility than its alternative. It matters to me that information confer certainty, because I am not someone who takes chances. This "certainty policy" reflects who I am, the kind of person I am. It is rationally permissible to apply the certainty policy in one's reasoning, and I choose to do so. Not everyone makes decisions according to the certainty policy, although it appears that most people do.[28]

Now, I apply the certainty policy in my practical reasoning not because information that confers certainty assures me of what the facts are (though it does assure me) but rather because I rationally value information that confers certainty over and above its evidentiary or probative value. So information that confers certainty is ellsbergian for me. The certainty policy is an ellsbergian policy.

I have already explained to you that when you asked me to imagine having received further information about the lottery outcome, the pattern in which the certainty policy applies to the four gambles is altered. Obtaining this new information would alter my rational evaluation of the four gambles in ways that are not exhausted by the new knowledge of the world I would have acquired. That is why I cannot use the backtracking Principle B in this situation, as I explained earlier. But since we disagree about whether I should change my epistemic policies to fit Principle B, or reject Principle B because it does not match my epistemic policies, I decided to give you a different example of an Ellsbergian policy. That is why I told you about my psychiatrist.

CASEY: Your story about the Hawaii vacation package is interesting, Jack. It has a familiar ring, but never mind. I'm glad you have found a way to cope with your neuroses. But I really cannot agree with the conclusions you want to draw. The trouble is, there are so many problems with the things you have said I do not know where to begin or how to fit all of the problems together into one nice, coherent objection. So, if you will forgive me, I will give you two objections. I admit they do not quite fit together.

My first objection is this. You just said that the certainty policy reflects who you are, the kind of person you are—so who can say it is irrational. Now that sounds to me like the kind of gibberish your shrink tells you. Of course it is irrational. To the extent that you act on the certainty policy, you are an irrational kind of person. The argument for that is easy: You will admit that choosing the act which maximizes expected utility will net you the most utility over the long haul. So a "maximizing policy" is bound to be rational. Your certainty policy conflicts with a maximizing policy—or at least can conflict with it and in the present case does conflict. So, your beloved certainty policy is bound to be irrational, however much it reflects who you are. All that means is that you are irrationally risk averse.

This objection applies equally well to your shrink counterexample. Obviously the policy your shrink recommended was irrational, because it, too, can conflict with a policy of utility maximization. In the present case it does conflict, since you went and paid a hard-earned five dollars just to get the chance to respond to the receipt of information in the way your shrink recommends. You would have gone on the vacation anyway. You just went on the vacation poorer.

My second objection is this. Think for a moment about your risk aversion. What happens is that you are made very ill at ease by risk. You find it stressful. Perhaps almost everyone does, which is why, as you point out, almost everyone follows a certainty policy. Now, when a bet is a certain winner, you like it partly because to back a certain winner relieves you of stress. It puts your mind at ease. This is not a monetary value, obviously, but we are dealing with expected utility, not with expected monetary value. Stress reduction is just a sort of premium you get for taking the bet you are certain to win. The rational way to take account of such a premium is to factor it in as added utility, boosting the utility you get from the monetary payoff alone. That raises the expected utility of the bet, and I venture to say that it raises it enough that you are really just maximizing expected utility after all. So your certainty policy is not incompatible with expected utility maximization after all, although it may be incompatible with "expected monetary gain" maximization.[29]

The same might be said about the policy your shrink recommended. If you really do get something out of the experience of confronting and conquering your neuroses, then the experience leads to a gain in utility. It can be thrown into the hopper along with the utility of saving money, the utility of enjoying yourself lying on a beach, and so forth. It will be just one more contributer to total utility. So perhaps your shrink's policy is not incompatible with expected utility maximization after all.

Now, my first objection gives me a very direct way to protect Principle B in the face of counterexamples like the ones you have suggested. I simply deny that the ellsbergian policies involved are rational policies. My second objection does not give me such a direct way to protect Principle B. What it suggests to me is that I should take back the argument I gave you, the argument aimed at showing your choices among bets were irrational. Perhaps they were not irrational at all, but one can only see that when one factors in components of utility other than monetary value when one calculates expected utility. Once I take back my original argument, Principle B will no longer be exposed to attack from that direction, as it were.

Now, as I said, these objections really do not fit together. I will try to think of a way to fit them together better. Meanwhile, what do you say to them? I hope you will not just take a cheap shot and point out that they are inconsistent.

JACK: I certainly will not take that cheap shot. I will address your objections separately. First, I really have doubts about your claim that acting so as to maximize expected utility will lead to one "accumulating" the greatest amount of utility over the long haul, as you put it. That may be a plausible claim if we are tacitly identifying accumulating utility with accumulating monetary winnings. When we use acts of accepting or rejecting bets as working examples of acts a person might perform, it is natural to make that identification. But if we are going to be serious about treating factors other than monetary value as components of total utility, as you suggest we do, then it is not at all obvious what "accumulating" utility can be. Let me explain what I mean.

Gambling houses succeed in accumulating money when they adopt the policy of trying to maximize expected value, with value reckoned in terms of money. In fact, when a gambler is able to play again and again with no practical limit on the size of bet she can make or the length of losing streak she can tolerate, an individual gambler who maximizes expected monetary value will accumulate money too. The world does behave the way the laws of large numbers say it will behave. If a person always acts so as to maximize expected value (expected monetary gain, for example), that person's sequence of actions probably will have a higher mean value (e.g., mean monetary gain) than any other sequence of actions probably would have—assuming the other sequence is not also one that always maximizes expected value. The strength of the "probably" in this formulation goes up as the sequence of actions gets longer and longer. Finally, it is obvious that if you perform the sequence of actions with the highest mean, or average, value per action, you will accumulate the most value as time goes by. For example, if you have been acting so as to maximize expected monetary gain, you will accumulate the most money as time goes by. Probably.

Defenders of subjective expected utility theory often give this "long run" argument as a reason for accepting their favorite decision rule. The type of value referred to in this version of the long-run argument is subjective utility. A person's subjective utility at a time is determined by the person's preferences (up to positive linear transformations of the utility scale). But everyone has changes of preference as time goes by. Some of these changes take place over a fairly long span of time. Some occur as we become adults rather than children, or as we become middle-aged rather than young adults. But short-term changes affect our preferences also. In fact, a great deal of experimental evidence shows that people's evaluations of how good or bad some outcome would be is differentially influenced by mood. Positive mood results in one regarding unpleasant events as relatively worse than one would regard them in a state of less positive mood.[30] Swings in mood, therefore, may be expected to stretch or compress parts of one's utility function. And swings of mood are a fact of life. Apparently, then, there is no sense to the idea of a single preference ranking for a person over time, at least when the length of time is considerable, and perhaps even when it is not.

It follows that subjective utiity is not like money or square footage of office space owned. It is not like one's knowledge of history, or the extent of one's travels, or the wine one has drunk. In each of these cases, something is accumulated over time, measurable in terms that remain roughly constant, even if the measure is hard to define, as with one's knowledge of history. But it seems there is a risk that with subjective utility, the only thing to "accumulate" over time might be real numbers, each a measure of one's preferences at some time or other, but none a measure of one's preferences at any other time, let alone at all other times. A risk is posed that no quantity of anything exists about which we can ask "How does one accumulate the greatest amount of this?" And if that is so, then there is no way to argue that the way to accumulate the greatest amount of this stuff is by maximizing expected utility case by case, action by action.

It may seem that there is an "ultrasubjectivist" reply. This ultra-subjectivist can insist that at any time when a choice situation arises, an agent need be concerned only with how to accumulate subjective utility as it arises from her preferences of the moment. This involves a sort of mul-tiple bookkeeping. At each time in the agent's life, her preference ranking will define an assignment of utilities to states of affairs that may figure as outcomes of actions. Normally one thinks of this process as restricted to what the agent is liable to contemplate at or around that time. Indeed, the agent may have no conception at all of what her options will be at times in the distant future, and she may have no preferences at all among many states of affairs that will at some future time be meaningful to her. The trick would be to treat the agent as indifferent among all such states of affairs.[31] This would enable her to get subjective utility values, and there will be such a thing as accumulating utility, though only utility as measured from one point of reference.

Every other time in the agent's life would be treated in similar fashion. From the perspective of any given point in time, there would be a well-defined possibility of accumulating more or less utility, as mea-sured just from that perspective. The agent must be assumed to think it desirable to accumulate utility in this ultrasubjectivist sense, a sense in which what the agent herself may want or may value later in life (perhaps hours later) plays no special role, except insofar as it is reflected in her preferences of the moment.

But surely, nobody really has so little regard for the wants, likes, and dislikes of her "future selves." Or, to make a slightly weaker point, if this is the only sense in which a certainty policy, or my shrink's recommended policy, is "irrational," then there is not much shame in being irrational. Most people would think it wise, prudent, clever—name your term of epistemic praise—to follow many policies that are "irrational" in such a dilute sense as this.

Now, here is the second point I want to make. The policy my shrink recommended *did* conflict with the policy of expected utility maximization. It is no good to find some element of value you can factor into "utility" and claim that all that is going on is expected utility maximization. Let me give you an analogy. You may have heard of the lawyer who argues as follows, before any evidence has been presented.[32] Either my client did it, in which case he is insane, the crime being so horrible, or my client didn't do it, in which case he is innocent. Either way, my client should not be convicted. A juror might well reject this argument on the following grounds. It matters *how* one reaches a decision concerning guilt or innocence. Procedure is important. The fact that one has heard evidence presented, and made a decision on the basis of that evidence, has an importance that goes beyond the probative value of the evidence. That is the sanctioned procedure, the right procedure. Therefore, information that has been presented in the proper manner, through the testimony of witnesses, is ellsbergian for a juror.

So the juror can foresee that when evidence has been presented, the evidence will show either that the defendant is not guilty, because it will not be probatively sufficient to establish guilt beyond a reasonable doubt, or else the evidence will show that the defendant did commit the crime, in which case it will follow that the defendant is insane and should be found not guilty by reason of insanity. Nevertheless, the juror can rationally decline, on procedural grounds, to decide guilt or innocence before any evidence has been presented. The lawyer wants the juror to reason in accord with clause (2) of Principle B, and the juror refuses to do so because the witness testimony that will be forthcoming will constitute ellsbergian information; it will have rational value that goes beyond its role as evidence for what the facts are. It will be evidence a jury ought to take into account because it is mandatory to take the testimony of witnesses into account.

Now, if you claim that this extra, ellsbergian, significance of evidence given in court can be factored in as just one more kind of utility, how would you factor it in? Which outcomes does this extra component of utility attach itself to? These is no sensible answer. What is going on here is that it matters *how* a decision is made, and this is not the same as an *outcome*.

We must avoid a possible confusion here. Consider the situation the juror is in before hearing any evidence, when the lawyer makes his speech. Now, even though this is not how juries really function, for simplicity assume that at this point in the proceeding the juror faces two different, though related, decisions. One is the decision whether the defendant did it (and is insane) or didn't do it (and should be acquitted). The other is the decision whether to go ahead with the trial, as opposed to setting the defendant free and going home for dinner. With respect to the first of these decisions, the juror feels very acutely the ellsbergian nature of the information that will be forthcoming if a trial is indeed held. That is why the juror refuses to call off the trial despite the lawyer's plea. This procedural consideration cannot be factored in as an element of utility attaching to some outcome of the decision whether to declare the defendant guilty or innocent. But with respect to the second of these decisions, it does make sense to factor in the prospective information from witnesses as an element of utility. Calling off the trial in the absence of testimony, since it violates procedural norms, has more disutility as a result. But the decision the lawyer is asking the juror to make is the first, not the second.

You should think of my adhering to my shrink's advice as a procedural consideration of sorts. When I eventually learn whether I have passed or failed the exam, and choose to go to Hawaii, I might not notice that the "procedural" consideration had played a role, because its terms had been satisfied. This would be like the juror not noticing at the *end* of the trial that a procedural constraint had been relevant, because by then the terms of the procedural constraint had been satisfied. *Before* I learn whether I have passed or failed, though, I am acutely aware of the procedural consideration, and it is my reason for paying a fee to postpone the decision.

Now, to return to our discussion of the lottery. You wanted to claim that I am risk averse, so that I prefer choices that minimize my risk-induced anxieties, and you wanted to factor this anxiety reduction into the utilities attached to the outcomes of my choices among the bets. This was so that you could argue that I am really just maximizing expected utility after all. I want to describe the situation differently. What I have called a "certainty policy" is analogous to the policy my shrink recommended, and the procedural rule the juror holds dear. Remember that I said "It matters to me that information confer certainty because

I am not someone who takes chances." I did not mean that as a comment on my anxieties, although you are right that I have anxieties connected with taking risks. I have a "procedural rule" to use when I evaluate decisions I must make under risk. I choose sure things when they are offered, unless the cost in utility is very high. I am a conservative. This is a matter of my politics in a very general sense. Perhaps it is even a matter of my ethics, though it seems closer to the mark to call it a political view. I would urge others to adopt a certainty policy, too. I think it makes sense. If my anxieties play a role in causing me to be this kind of person, it still does not follow that having those anxieties *is the same thing as* being this kind of person.

CASEY: The truth is, the argument I laid out for you to show that you made an irrational selection of bets seemed absolutely persuasive to me. Frankly, I am not sure how to shake you from your story about "procedure" and such. The only approach I can think of is this. I am willing to present a different set of hypothetical choices, also involving gambles. I suspect you will have a reaction to this set of choices unlike my own. But at the moment I cannot see how your analysis of the Allais gambles can be extended to this new set of choices among bets. Perhaps we can meet again tomorrow, if it's a nice day, and discuss the matter.

JACK: Sure.

Daniel Ellsberg's Problem

The next day Jack and Casey met again for a walk through the park. As he had promised, Casey presented Jack with another problem about bets.

CASEY: For a start, Jack, imagine that you are offered two simple bets. One bet is on the outcome of randomly drawing a ball from an urn containing 50 red balls and 50 black balls. You get $10 if a red ball is drawn, and you lose $5 if a black ball is drawn. The other bet is the same, except for the fact that the urn from which the ball will be drawn contains 100 red and black balls in an unknown proportion—unknown to you, that is. In each case, the probability of a red ball being drawn is 0.5. My own view is that a rational gambler would rate these bets exactly equal. For example, she would trade the right to make one of them for the right to make the other without demanding any additional payment to make the deal fair, and without thinking she really ought to throw in a little something to make the deal fair. Of course, both bets are outrageously favorable to the bettor. Whoever is offering them is very silly. But they are exactly equally outrageously favorable.

Given the things you have said about your taste for conservative policies to guide your decision-making, I suspect you will disagree with me. But I cannot see exactly why. Perhaps you would tell me your evaluation of these two hypothetical bets.

JACK: I think I see where you're headed, Casey. But I'm willing to take things one step at a time, as you evidently want us to do. My evaluation of the two bets you just described is this: I would take the first bet but not the second, even though I agree that I would have a 0.5 chance of winning in either case. The 0.5 probability I would assign to winning the first bet arises from a real random process in the world, whereas the same probability in the second bet merely reflects my ignorance as to which random process is at work. I know that the first urn has a propensity to yield red balls a certain percentage of the time—to be specific, half the time, on average. But I have no such knowledge about the second urn. The second urn might have a 50–50 ratio of red to black balls, just as in the first bet. But it also might have a 2-to-98 ratio, or a 77-to-33 ratio, or a 40-to-60 ratio, and so on for every possible ratio. Possible, that is, given the constraint that there are 100 balls in some red-black mixture or other. So I do not know the propensity of the second urn to yield red balls. It is true that whatever that propensity is, it is just as likely that it is favorable to me as that it is unfavorable to me, but that is nothing but a measure of my complete ignorance of what type of red ball generator is sitting there before me. In the case of the first urn, by contrast, I am absolutely sure what type of red ball generator is before me. It is the type one would describe by saying it has a 0.5 propensity for delivering up a red ball. The urn behaves that way due to the mixture of red and black balls it contains. This is a property of the urn, just as much as its color or shape is a property. I don't know how the second urn behaves, and I can put a measure on my ignorance: 0.5.

Other things being more or less equal, I prefer to take risks when, in this sense, I really know what they are. I prefer to know what random process I am dealing with. I like to call this policy "the real propensity policy." I would argue that the real propensity policy assigns a rational value to information about what real propensity is at work, and that this rational value goes beyond the probative value of that information, where by "the probative value of the information" I mean the likelihood it confers upon some hypothesis about what the facts are, a hypothesis such as "a red ball will be drawn."

But I am getting ahead of myself. I do not expect you to see the motivation for all the claims I just made, at least not yet. I guess I got excited when I saw that you were going to bring up these examples. You see, Casey, these are the kind of examples Daniel Ellsberg described quite some time ago. When I chose the term "ellsbergian" to describe certain kinds of information, it was these examples I had in mind as paradigms. In particular, I had in mind the real propensity policy as a paradigm of an ellsbergian policy. That may be slightly misleading, since Ellsberg himself did not recommend the real propensity policy in response to the examples he described. But now I really am getting ahead of myself. Please go ahead with your questions.

CASEY: I see I have walked into a hornets' nest here, Jack. I had no idea you had been thinking about Ellsberg's examples all these years. Maybe you were doing it when I thought you were napping in the sun. Anyway, let me tell you about another betting problem, related to the first one but more complicated. This set of hypothetical bets will provide me with the setup for an argument, an argument very similar to the one I gave you to show that your choices among the Allais gambles were irrational. Eventually what I want to do is explore with you whether you have reservations about my new argument similar to your reservations about my previous

TABLE 1.5.   Casey's table of the actions and possible
outcomes in one of D. Ellsberg's decision problems.

	30 balls	60 balls		
	(Red)	(Black)	or	(Yellow)
Action 1 yields	$100	$0		$0
Action 2 yields	$0	$100		$0
Action 3 yields	$100	$0		$100
Action 4 yields	$0	$100		$100

argument. I will tell you in advance that the argument I intend to give you strikes me as very compelling, just as the Businessman Argument strikes me as compelling. But now I'm the one who is getting ahead of himself. Let's start with the hypothetical bets. As I now know you know, these bets were first described and discussed by Daniel Ellsberg.

Here Casey produced another of his neatly lettered tables (table 1.5), allegedly to "help Jack fix the terms of the bets in mind." Then Casey continued, explaining the meaning of the entries in the table—although Jack already knew what they meant, and already had a thought-out reaction to them.

CASEY: I'm sure you are familiar with these four bets, Jack, but just to make sure we are on the same page, here is the problem for you to consider. Suppose an urn is filled with 90 balls, 30 of which are red (R) and 60 of which are black (B) or yellow (Y), in an unknown mixture. One ball is to be drawn at random with a payoff of either $100 or $0, depending on the "action" (the gamble) selected and the color of the drawn ball, as shown in the table. This is your problem. First choose between action 1, to bet on red, and action 2, to bet on black. Then choose between action 3, to bet on red or yellow, and action 4, to bet on black or yellow.

As you can see, Jack, the table specifies what payoff you get from any given action if a red ball is chosen, or a black ball, or a yellow ball. Now, do you prefer action 1 to action 2, or vice versa? Do you prefer action 3 to action 4, or vice versa?

JACK: I prefer action 1 to action 2, and I prefer action 4 to action 3. I have no doubt at all about these choices, although I can imagine a person taking some time to decide, and perhaps being a bit unsure even then, given the complexity of the bets. But I have thought about the matter before. Let me explain.[33]

I know that 30 of the 90 balls in the urn are red, so I know that the urn has a propensity for yielding a red ball one-third of the time on average. So, if I choose action 1, I have a one-third chance of winning $100. And this probability reflects a real propensity. In the case of action 2, on the other hand, all that I know is that there are somewhere between 0 and 60 black balls in the urn. If one of them is drawn, I win $100; otherwise, I win nothing. I do not know the propensity of the urn to deliver up a winning ball. The one-third probability I assign to winning is a reflection of this lack of knowledge. Therefore, my real propensity policy dictates that I choose action 1 over action 2. "Other things are equal"; the probability of my winning is the same in both cases. But the information I have in the case of action 1 has a value to me that goes beyond its probative force. I know the actual propensity of the urn to generate red balls when "sampled"; I know something important about the way it behaves. Therefore, according to my real propensity policy, I ought to choose action 1.

The situation is the same in the cases of actions 3 and 4. In the case of action 4, I know that exactly 60 of the 90 balls are black or yellow, and therefore I know that the urn has a two-thirds propensity for yielding a winning ball, whereas in the case of action 3, all that I know is that an unknown number of balls between 30 and 90 are red or yellow, and thus are "winners." The probabilities of winning are the same for action 4 and action 3: two-thirds in each case. But the information I have in connection with action 4 has a value to me that goes beyond its mere value as evidence for what will happen. It reflects a real propensity, and that is very important to me when I am deciding what to do. The information I have in connection with action 3 also supports a two-thirds probability, but this probability is a measure of my ignorance of the urn's propensity to deliver a winning ball, not a measure of that propensity itself. So I much prefer action 4 to action 3.

CASEY: I simply cannot accept the things you have said about your "real propensity policy." I have been trying to think how to argue against it. One strategy would be to go ahead and tell you my argument that parallels the argument I gave you in the Allais case. My argument shows that the pair of choices you have made here is irrational. I think I can see how you would reply, but perhaps we should go through the exercise. So here is my argument.

Either you will learn that a yellow ball has been drawn (call this epistemic state e_2), or else you will learn that a red or a black ball has been drawn (call this epistemic state e_3). Assume that you learn that a yellow ball has been drawn; you are in epistemic state e_2. Then you should be indifferent between having chosen action 1 and having chosen action 2. Either choice will have won you nothing at all. Likewise, you should be indifferent between having chosen action 3 and having chosen action 4. Either choice will have earned you $100.

Now assume that you learn that a red ball or a black ball has been chosen; you are in epistemic state e_3. You then know that having chosen action 1 has given you exactly the same winnings as having chosen action 3 (although without further information you would not know what those winnings are). Analogously, you know that having chosen action 2 has given you exactly the same winnings as having chosen action 4. So, if you are in e_3, consistency requires you (a) to prefer having chosen action 1 to having chosen action 2 and to prefer having chosen action 3 to having chosen action 4, or (b) to prefer having chosen action 2 to having chosen action 1 and to prefer having chosen action 4 to having chosen action 3, or (c) to be indifferent between having chosen action 1 or 2 and indifferent between having chosen action 3 or 4. *Certainly* you ought not prefer having chosen action 1 over action 2 but action 4 over action 3. Therefore, either you will be in e_2 and it will be a matter of indifference which choices you made, or you will be in e_3 and you will be glad to have made some set of choices other than action 1 over action 2 and action 4 over action 3. Since e_2 and e_3 are the only possibilities, your pair of choices was irrational.

The argument I just gave you *almost* follows clause (1) of Principle B. It does not quite follow it, since I included the option that if you were in e_3 you might be indifferent between having chosen action 1 or 2, and indifferent between having chosen action 3 or 4. It would be easy to add to Principle B some language saying that if in both e_2 and e_3 you should be indifferent which action you had performed, then in fact, in e_1, it should be a matter of indifference which action you perform. I did not include this language in Principle B just to simplify it, although Savage did include an equivalent clause in his sure-thing principle.

I would like to hear what you think of this argument, Jack. I find it compelling, as I said. If you don't, please tell me why.

JACK: What I have to say here is very similar to what I said about the argument you gave me in the case of the lottery form of the Allais problem. Perhaps one point will suffice to illustrate what I mean. When I do not yet know what color ball will be drawn—when I am in what we are calling epistemic state e_1—action 1 has a "real propensity policy advantage" over action 2, and action 4 has a real propensity policy advantage over action 3. I have explained what I mean by that. Now, suppose I am in e_1, but contemplating what I will judge that I should have done when I "look backward" from e_2 or from e_3. In particular, suppose I am contemplating how things will seem to me when I look backward from e_3. Of course, I do not know that I will be in e_3 rather than e_2, but your argument requires that I go through the exercise for both e_2 and e_3. When I contemplate being in e_3, I am narrowing the range of epistemic alternatives—it is ruled out that a yellow ball is chosen. The alternatives are that a red ball is chosen or a black ball is chosen. I know the urn has a one-third propensity to yield red balls, and has some propensity or other from zero to two-thirds to yield black balls. In each case the probability is the same: one-third. But the one-third probability of a red ball being chosen reflects a real propensity of the system with which I am dealing.

This means that when I contemplate being in e_3, I give a "real propensity policy advantage" to having chosen action 3 over action 4. Since neither action 3 nor action 4 has any advantage over the other if a yellow ball is drawn, and I wind up in e_2, clause (1) of Principle B tells me to prefer action 3 to action 4. *In fact*, action 4 has a "real propensity policy advantage" over action 3. The reasoning required by Principle B trades on an epistemic illusion produced by imagining that the set of epistemic alternatives has been narrowed. So, if I accept Principle B and therefore accept your argument, it will be because I have done my reasoning from imaginary epistemic perspectives in a way that falsifies the way my real propensity policy actually applies to the choices I must make.

CASEY: I think you're right about that, Jack. So I guess I need to confront your real propensity policy head on. Let me put it this way. In the case of the policy your shrink recommended, and even in the case of your certainty policy, you gave me some reasons to believe that the policies were rationally acceptable—policies a rational person could adopt without forfeiting her rationality—even though someone could choose not to adopt them, again without forfeiting her rationality. But I cannot see why your real propensity policy amounts to anything more than a whim.

You just *like* probabilities that reflect real propensities. You have given me no reason at all to believe that it is even prima facie rational of you to do so.

JACK: You are right that I owe you an argument for the rational acceptability of the real propensity policy. Let me try to give one.

Suppose I am considering hiring employees for my small store. I have a choice of two different agencies from which to hire my new employee. Agency A helps place people with past criminal records. They make the record of the prospective employee available to the employer, together with an estimate, made by an expert, on how likely the person is to steal. I pick out a candidate, and in the case of that candidate the expert judges that, given the candidate's personality profile, he has a 0.03 chance of stealing from an employer. Agency A supplies me with the expert's evaluation, and a full explanation of how the expert arrived at his evaluation.

Agency B handles a wide variety of potential employees and is committed to keeping their personal histories confidential. Thus, if I am to hire someone from Agency B and I want to know how likely it is that the person will steal, the best I can do is get the FBI crime statistics on the group of people with the same demographic profile as those handled by Agency B (assume I know enough about the "typical" Agency B client to be able to make this match). Suppose I discover that 0.03 percent of people in this group steal from employers.

I know that if I hire the person from Agency A, that person will have a 0.03 propensity of stealing from me. In the case of Agency B, all I know is that, given all the people I might hire from that agency, there is a 0.03 chance that the person I hire will steal. I might get someone with no propensity to steal, and I might get an inveterate thief.

I prefer to hire someone from Agency A. The information I receive from Agency A is more valuable to me than the information I receive from Agency B. I have a "tolerance threshold" for dishonesty in my employees. If a person has a propensity to steal that is greater than, say, 0.2, I will refuse to hire the person. Given the precise propensity information provided by Agency A, I can rest assured that my tolerance threshold has not been crossed. This is not true of the person from Agency B. I know next to nothing about that person's character. Moreover, in the case of the person from Agency B, there is a great deal of information about the person's propensity to steal that is potentially available to others. So people who know more about the matter than I know—people who know the person's real propensity to steal and who are not relying on mere actuarial statistics as I must do—could exploit this knowledge in many ways to my disadvantage (the simplest being to seek this person out as a confederate to rob my store).[34]

When it comes to hiring an employee, then, I do not find knowledge of the actuarial probabilities gleaned from FBI statistics as useful as knowledge of a real propensity. One can easily imagine similar reasons for having this preference in other situations. Thus it is reasonable of me to have the general policy of seeking knowledge of real propensities rather than knowledge of mere actuarial probabilities, and it is reasonable of me to put more weight, in my decision-making, on probabilities that reflect propensities.

I realize, Casey, that you may agree that it is easy to imagine reasons for adopting the real propensity policy in the rich and complex context of the practical decisions we make in our lives, but still deny that there is any reason for me to apply this policy when deciding which bets to take in Ellsberg's problem. You could claim that in the case of those bets, my decision is not interwoven with other decisions in the same way.

One reply I could make is that it is most rational for me to have a *general* policy of distinguishing probabilities that reflect real propensities from probabilities that do not. So it is rational for me to apply this policy whenever I make a decision, even if there are particular cases where having that policy can't be locally justified. This sort of defense of having a fully general policy is the sort of defense one finds given by rule utilitarians for applying moral rules in particular cases where, on its own, the principle of utility would not justify applying the rule. It is hard to live by a policy that is peppered with exceptions, especially when the exceptions are not specified in advance. But although this line of defense is available, there are other reasons to think that it is rational of me to apply my real propensity policy in the case of Ellsberg's bets.

Whenever someone is offered a bet in a situation where there is more information to be had in the world about the random process that determines the payoff of the bet than the person being asked to make the bet is in possession of, it is reasonable for the person being asked to make the bet to worry that someone else has that information and somehow can exploit it. Thus it is reasonable to devalue that bet relative to a similar bet where there is no such information. It is easy to pretend that betting propositions described in theoretical examples are, in a sense, not really bets. Real bets are made by real people, and real people sometimes do exploit privileged information to the disadvantage of a bettor. It is fine to say: "But you must think of these as idealized betting situations, where it could not happen that someone knows a real propensity you do not know, thus entailing a risk that you will get ripped off." My answer is that I cannot do that. I have said that I am a conservative. Well, conservatives are cynics. I cannot turn off the faucet of cynicism merely because I am reading a learned article. I claim that this is a rational option. Let me put it another way. If you say that in Ellsberg's bets I am to imagine that it simply does not matter if I lack propensity information that is there to be had, then I say I cannot imagine them to be *bets*.

CASEY: I have to tell you, Jack, that I have never heard anything so outrageous. Nothing could be easier than considering Ellsberg's bets as idealized in such a way that real people with all their foibles have nothing to do with the situation. But I know it will do no good to keep insisting on that. So I will give you another objection. It has the form of a slippery-slope argument. To make it as simple as possible, let's return to the first betting situation we discussed in connection with Ellsberg's problem. You had to decide whether to bet on a red ball being drawn from an urn containing 50 red and 50 black balls, or bet on a red ball being drawn from an urn containing 100 balls, in some unknown mixture of red and black.

First, let me modify the problem in the following way. You must choose between betting on a red ball being drawn from an urn with a 50–50 mixture of red and black balls, winning $10 if a red ball is drawn, losing $5 if a black ball is drawn, or betting on a red ball being drawn from an urn with an unknown mixture of red and black, with the same payoffs. But as I now want to tell the story, the urn containing the unknown mixture of red and black balls has the following history. It was taken at random from a room in which there were 100 urns, each of them containing one of the possible combinations of red and black balls, from 1 red and 100 black through 100 red and 1 black. Given your real propensity policy, I assume that this added information does not change your view; you would take the first bet, where you know the exact ratio of red to black balls in the urn. Is that right?

JACK: Yes.

CASEY: Now let me make a further modification in my description of the second bet. There is a room with 100 urns configured as I just described.

But no particular urn is singled out and brought forward. If you decide to take the bet, a person who is administering the process will walk around the room, randomly stick his hand into one of the urns, and bring out a ball. Notice, Jack, that what you have in this situation is a big container—the room—in which there are 5,000 red balls and 5,000 black balls, although the balls are confined to a funny-shaped region within the room—a region shaped like 100 urns. Now I will admit that this is not the same as having 5,000 red balls and 5,000 black balls all sloshing around together in a big container. But is it not a "device" with a known real propensity for yielding up a red ball—namely 0.5? So, given your real propensity policy, shouldn't you be indifferent between this bet and the bet on the single urn containing 50 red and 50 black balls?

JACK: I suppose so. I would want to know a little more about this allegedly impartial administrator, though. But I will drop that concern, since you are outraged by such things.

CASEY: Fine. Now suppose that after you have made your bet—and let us assume you have decided to bet on an urn from the room—the administrator merely points to an urn, which is then carried to the center of the room, where a ball is drawn from it. This changes nothing of substance, does it? You would still be indifferent between this bet and the bet on an urn known to contain a 50–50 mixture of red and black balls?

JACK: I would still be indifferent.

CASEY: Now we are at the end of the slippery slope, Jack. If you would be indifferent between the two bets in the case I just described, surely it would make no difference to you if the administrator *first* picked an urn at random, had it moved to the center of the room, and *then* asked you to choose between betting on a red ball being drawn from this urn and betting on a red ball being drawn from the urn with a 50–50 ratio of red and black balls. But now the second bet, the bet on the urn taken from the room, is exactly the same as the original second bet. You would be betting on an urn with an unknown mixture of red and black balls. Surely you agree that it cannot matter whether you place your bet before or after the administrator points to an urn in the room.

JACK: Of course it matters. I would not take the second bet in the last form you have described. I would be betting on a drawing *from a different object*. I would be betting on the color of a ball to be drawn from an urn with an unknown mixture of red and black balls. I would not know the propensity of this object to yield red balls. In the version of your story immediately before this one, I would be betting that a red ball would be yielded up by an object whose propensity to yield red balls was known to me—a room with a 0.5 propensity to yield red balls. It makes no difference that the urn I am being asked to bet on at the final stage of your slippery slope was, as it were, a piece of the room that has now been torn loose.

I am not sure how Ellsberg himself would have answered your questions. Let me explain.

Daniel Ellsberg first described the problem we have been discussing in 1961.[35] With respect to the four bets in your table, Ellsberg hypothesized that people who prefer action 1 to action 2 do so because, in his terms, their information in the case of action 1 is "less ambiguous" than their information in the case of action 2. This is how he describes the notion of the "ambiguity" of information:

> This judgment of the ambiguity of one's information, of the over-all credibility of one's composite estimates, of one's confidence in them, cannot be expressed in terms of relative likelihoods of events (if it could, it would simply affect the final, compound probabilities). Any scrap of evidence bearing on relative likelihood should already be represented in those estimates. But having exploited knowledge, guess, rumor, assumption, advice, to arrive at a final judgment that one event is more likely than another or that they are equally likely, one can still stand back from this process and ask: "How much, in the end, is all this worth? How much do I really know about the problem? How firm a basis for choice, for appropriate decision and action, do I have?"[36]

It is not clear whether Ellsberg thought of "ambiguity" as an epistemic property of information, a component in the overall probative value of information as evidence for what the facts are, or as a non-epistemic factor contributing to the "worth" of the information (his term) as an ingredient in one's specifically *practical* reasoning, one's deciding what to *do*. On the first interpretation, ambiguity affects the rationality of a choice of action only by affecting the reasonableness of accepting certain relevant beliefs. It's just that ambiguity is a separate ingredient in the mix, separate from likelihood. On the second interpretation, ambiguity affects the wisdom of using the information in practical reasoning, but *not* because it affects the probative value of the information. Most commentators on Ellsberg's work have taken him the first way. I take him the second way.

I do not think the term "ambiguity" was a happy choice. What is at issue can be the fact that some information reflects real propensities while other information does not. Or it can be that some information makes possible an especially "conservative" betting strategy, as we saw in connection with the Allais Problem. There are further possibilities. It seems to me unhelpful to lump all these phenomena together as examples of "ambiguous" information.

Ellsberg experimented to see whether people confronting his bets made the choices expected utility theory dictates, or whether they made the choices I prefer. Others have made similar tests.[37] By a large margin, people prefer action 1 to action 2, but prefer action 4 to action 3. I conjecture that they are applying a real propensity policy, though covertly. This has not been studied experimentally, but I believe it should be.

I am unsure how Ellsberg would have replied to your slippery-slope argument, Casey, because I am unsure exactly how to apply his concept of "ambiguity." I suppose he might think your sequence of examples was "nonambiguity preserving"—in which case your slippery-slope argument might have troubled him. It does not trouble me.[38]

It was obvious to both Jack and Casey that they were unlikely to reach agreement in this matter. Both promised to think a bit more about it. They decided to meet again the next day.

Simpson's Paradox

When Jack and Casey met the next day, Casey was a bit annoyed.

CASEY: I've been thinking, Jack, and here is what I have decided. You may be right that some information is ellsbergian for people who must make decisions. And you may be right that as a result of this, there can be rational ellsbergian policies for evaluating decisions. But I must tell you that the three examples you have given me, and worked through in detail—your "certainty policy," your "real propensity policy," and the policy your shrink recommended to you—are not well chosen if you want to convince others of your view. Perhaps they are rational policies, perhaps not. You concede that they are optional. My own view is that they belong in the category of cognitive illusions. You, and—at least in the case of the certainty policy and the real propensity policy—perhaps many other people, are firmly intuitively persuaded that the choices these policies dictate are correct. There may be some psychological explanation for these cognitive illusions, just as psychologists have proposed explanations for visual illusions that are nearly universally experienced, such as "illusory contours." But the illusory contours are not really there, and the added "value" that you intuitively judge should be added to, say, a bet that is a certain winner is not really there either. By "added value" I mean value over and above the value deriving from expected utility. The fact that a cognitive illusion is widely experienced does not give it any credentials as an element of rationality. People, of whom I am one, who have not chosen your ellsbergian policies to guide their decision-making will not be persuaded by an argument that one of these policies is the "conservative" thing to do, let alone by an argument that it is the "cynical" thing to do, or that it is a good way to make choices in order to battle neuroses. This includes people who, like you, feel the intuitive "pull" of the policies. It is possible to take an objective view of oneself and recognize that suboptimal, even thoroughly irrational, approaches to decision-making may sometimes seem intuitively correct. It would be much better if you could give me an example of an ellsbergian policy that would be accepted by most thoughtful people as fully rational.

JACK: I have been thinking very much the same thing, Casey. So I will tell you about a puzzling situation I came across a while ago, and I will tell you how I finally sorted it out. I think this will give you the kind of example you want. We will need pencil and paper for this. Perhaps I can borrow some of those cards you like to write your tables of bets on.

TABLE 1.6.   Table illustrating the increased cancer risk from smoking (Jack's first version).

	Smokers	Nonsmokers
Cancer	49,501	9,980
No cancer	50,499	890,020

This is the puzzle I encountered. It is quite well known, as I learned, and is called Simpson's Paradox. As you know, I once enjoyed smoking. I wondered whether I should quit. The only possible consequence of smoking I cared about was whether or not smoking would increase my chances of getting cancer. I did some reading on the topic, and found the data I'll write out for you here (table 1.6).

I concluded that if I smoked, my chances of getting cancer were $49,501/100,000 = 0.49501$, whereas if I didn't smoke my chances were only $9,980/900,000 = 0.01109$. I concluded that I was better off not smoking by a factor of about 45 to 1.

Then I came across an article in a magazine. I have since learned that it was a hoax, but I did not realize that at the time. So let's pretend it was true. The article said that postmortem genetic tests were performed on the very same population described in the statistics I just showed you. It was discovered that some members of the population had a certain gene, gene X, and others did not. When the researchers looked at the cancer rates of smokers and nonsmokers with and without gene X, they discovered that the data broke down as I'll write out for you here (table 1.7).

So I was confronted with two different sets of statistical information about exactly the same people.[39] I wondered what to make of it. Now,

TABLE 1.7.   The fraudulent gene X data Jack found.

	Smoke + X	Smoke w/o X	No-smoke + X	No-smoke w/o X
Cancer	49,500	1	990	8990
No cancer	49,500	999	10	890,010
Total	99,000	1,000	1,000	899,000

as it happened, the article I was reading went on to suggest how I should analyze the situation. I will set out that analysis in the form of an argument with exactly the structure of the arguments you have been showing me, so that it will be clear where Principle B plays a role, and so that it will be clear why an ellsbergian policy of mine eventually led me to reject the argument. Here is the argument.

Pretend that someone eventually discovers a way for people to learn whether or not they have gene X—a way to learn this while they are still alive, by noninvasive genetic testing methods. Clearly you (i.e., the reader of the article) should have this test done, learn whether you have gene X, and then apply the statistics just given. In fact, though, you need not wait for the genetic test to be developed. Even without knowing whether you have gene X, you can reason as follows.

> (1) Either I will learn that I have gene X (call this epistemic state e_2), or I will learn that I do not have gene X (call this epistemic state e_3). I can be sure of this, stipulating that the test will be developed and stipulating that I will have the test performed on me.
> (2) Assume that I learn that I have gene X (that is, assume that I am in e_2). Then, if I smoke, my chance of cancer is $49,500/99,000 = 0.5$. If I don't smoke, my chance of cancer is $990/1000 = 0.99$. Obviously, if I learn that I have gene X, I should much prefer having chosen to be a smoker.
> (3) Assume that I learn that I do not have gene X (that is, assume that I am in epistemic state e_3). Then, if I smoke, my chance of cancer is $1/1000 = .001$. If I don't smoke, my chance of cancer is $8,990/899,000 = 0.01$. Obviously, if I learn that I don't have gene X, I should prefer having chosen to be a smoker.
> (4) Now, since I have surveyed the only possibilities for what I will learn about having gene X, and in either case it would be clear to me that I should have been a smoker, the rational decision for me to make now (in epistemic state e_1) is to smoke.

You will observe, Casey, that the rule of inference upon which this argument rests is Principle B, in particular clause (2), the "strong dominance" clause.

I was shocked by this argument, and amazed by the gene X statistics. But I decided to take the statistics at face value, having no special reason to doubt them. So I directed my attention to analyzing the argument. To explain my analysis, I need to tell you something about the way I make use of this kind of statistical information in my reasoning.

Take the first table of statistics, the one that does not mention gene X. That table provides information about the frequency of occurrence of a certain property in a class. The property is "getting cancer," and the class is the group of people studied. The table also provides information about the frequency of occurrence of the property in each of two subclasses of the group of people—those who are smokers and those who are not. Let us say that a set of mutually exclusive, jointly exhaustive subclasses of a given class is a *partition* of the class. We can say that the property "being a smoker" partitions the class of people in the study, into the subclass of those who have the property and the subclass of those who do not. Let A be a class. Let C be a property that partitions the class, into A.C and A.not-C (A.C = the class of members of A possessing C). We can write the frequency of a property C in a class A as P(A,C). The reason I use the letter *P* here is that if the statistics have been properly gathered, I treat this frequency as an estimate of the probability with which the property tends to occur among generally similar subjects. Finally, let us say that a property C, which partitions a class A, is statistically relevant to attribute B within A when P(A.C, B) is not identical to P(A,B). It is easy to see that, according to these definitions, the property "being a smoker" is statistically relevant to the attribute "getting cancer" within the class of people studied.[40]

Now, the reason I gave all those definitions, Casey, is to enable me to explain how I solve a certain problem that often comes up. I may know the frequency of occurrence of some property in a class, but what I really want to know is the probability that some one member of the class has the property. I want to know how to transfer probabilities from classes to single objects, when the objects are members of the classes. The simplest rule is just to say that the frequency of the property in the class (thought of as a good estimate of the probability that "such things" have the property) equals the probability that the object in question has the property.

But anyone who takes this approach must face up to the fact that objects belong to many different classes. The property in question may have different frequencies of occurrence in different classes to which the object belongs. So which class does one choose for a "reference class"? Nothing in probability theory can answer that question. What we need, essentially, is what Carnap called "a methodological rule for applying inductive logic." Now, the fact is that I have not found a policy that I am sure always will enable me to pick out the correct reference class. I must settle for a policy that will enable me to choose *the best reference class relative to the information I have at a given time.*

Now, I do not want my reference class to be either too narrow or too broad. What I mean by that is that I want to narrow my reference class as far as possible, but not in statistically irrelevant ways. Here is the policy I use.

> *Policy C (for "Carnap"):* When I choose a reference class to which I am going to refer a given single case, I ask if there is any statistically relevant way *known to me* to subdivide that class. If there is, I use the narrower class resulting from that subdivision. If there is not, I avoid making the reference class any narrower.

Policy C is ellsbergian. When I receive new information, the information may enable me to pick some new reference classes to enable me to "transfer" probabilities (as estimated by frequencies) "onto" single objects. Really I should say "single events" here, since the probabilities I am seeking are the probabilities that these events will occur. The same new evidence may provide me with evidence for what the facts are; it may have probative value. But the role played by new information in helping me refine my reference classes is not the same as the role of that information as evidence for what the facts are.

Many people would agree with me that Policy C is a good way to select reference classes. And even those who prefer a different policy would be very unlikely to denigrate Policy C as a mere "cognitive illusion." So I have given you what you asked me to give—an example of an ellsbergian policy that would be widely accepted as rational. Now let me explain how Policy C made it easy for me to debunk the argument I found in the magazine.

Let's call the state of knowledge I was in when I was making my decision whether to smoke e_1. In line with the terminology of Principle B, let e_2 be the state of knowledge I would be in if I were to learn I have gene X, and let e_3 be the state of knowledge I would be in if I were to learn that I did not have gene X. While I am in e_1, Policy C dictates that I should use the reference classes "person in the study group who smokes" and "person in the study group who does not smoke." Of course, I was not in the study group, but I assume, inductively, that since the people in the study group were "typical," I can reason as though I were a member.

When I do that, I find that for a single member of the "smoker" group, the cancer probability is 0.49501. Repeating this exercise for the "non-smoker" group, I get a cancer rate of 0.01109. This is how I reached my original conclusion that I was much better off not smoking.

The argument in the article I read, at least as I paraphrased it for you, asked me to first contemplate learning I had gene X, that is to say, being in state e_2, and then to contemplate learning I did not have gene X, that is to say, being in state e_3. Now, when I imagined myself learning that I had gene X, I reasoned in exactly the way I just described, except that in e_2 my new information required me to shift to new, narrower, reference classes. This is required by Policy C. The cancer probabilities at which I arrived when I had changed reference classes differed substantially from the probabilities I computed while in e_1—that is, while in my actual state of knowledge. The same thing occurred when I imagined learning that I did not have gene X, that is, when I imagined being in state e_3.

Now, as you can see, Casey, these altered—narrowed—reference classes are not the reference classes I should, in fact, use in order to calculate the cancer risk associated with smoking. The argument in the magazine was invalid. Simpson's Paradox is not a paradox at all. It is a fallacy.

CASEY: I follow your argument, Jack, but I have a worry about it. I won't contest your Policy C, except to note that not everyone would accept it. You are right, though, that it is a principle that many people would accept as rational, and it probably is fair to say that those who would not accept it as rational would characterize this as a difference of philosophical opinion. My worry is this: If the argument you read in the magazine is invalid, as you suggest, there should be plausible counterexamples. I can't think of one, can you?

JACK: Well, I can think of a counterexample to a very similar argument, although it is an argument that relies on clause (1) of Principle B, rather than clause (2). Let me describe the argument, and the counterexample, and we can discuss what it does and does not show.

Suppose I learn that there is a chemical Y that alters the relation between smoking and cancer. I learn about this chemical while I still know only the original statistics relating smoking and cancer. For the purposes of this example, assume that I never read the magazine article about gene X. I do, however, learn that the effects on people who ingest or absorb chemical Y were studied in exactly the same population used

TABLE 1.8.   Jack's "chemical Y" data.

	Smoke + Y	Smoke w/o Y	No smoke + Y	No smoke w/o Y
Cancer	49,500	1	500	9,480
No cancer	49,500	999	500	889,520
Total	99,000	1,000	1,000	899,000

to generate the first set of statistics relating smoking and cancer that I read. Although none of them realized it, some of these people were exposed to chemical Y and some were not. Later investigation determined which people fell into which subclass. The investigators generated the data I'll now write out for you (table 1.8).

Now, here is an argument: Let e_1 be the epistemic state I am in when I am deliberating whether to smoke. Let e_2 be the epistemic state I would be in if I were to learn I had somehow absorbed some chemical Y. Let e_3 be the epistemic state I would be in if I learned I had not absorbed any chemical Y. Let us stipulate that I am going to be tested for the presence of substances which are absolutely reliable indicators whether a person has or has not absorbed chemical Y—no false positives and no false negatives.

So, I will be in e_2 or else I will be in e_3. If I am in e_2 in the future, that is, if I learn I have absorbed chemical Y, then my cancer risk will be 0.5 if I have been smoking and also will be 0.5 if I have not been smoking. Therefore, if I come to be in epistemic state e_2, I should be indifferent whether I chose to smoke or chose not to smoke. If I am in e_3 in the future, that is, if I learn that I positively have not absorbed any chemical Y, then if I have been smoking, my cancer risk is 0.001, whereas if I have not been smoking, my cancer risk is about 0.01. Therefore, if I come to be in epistemic state e_3, I should prefer having chosen to smoke over having chosen not to smoke. Applying clause (1) of Principle B, I conclude that now, when I am in epistemic state e_1, I should choose to smoke.

Now, suppose I go and get tested for the presence of chemical Y. My test is positive; I learn that I have absorbed chemical Y. This new information obliges me to shift to a narrower reference class, just as I imagined it doing when I was only imagining learning I had absorbed chemical Y. It becomes a matter of indifference to me whether I smoke, since my cancer risk is the same whether I smoke or do not smoke. Before I acquired this information, the available statistics led me to prefer not to smoke. To simplify the situation, but in a way that affects nothing essential, assume I never learn anything else in my life that is statistically relevant to my risk of cancer if I smoke, or don't smoke.

Here, then, is my situation. For part of my life, the evidence available to me shows that I should not smoke. Eventually I acquire new information that shows I should be indifferent whether I smoke or do not smoke. *At no time in my life does the evidence available to me show that I should prefer to smoke.* But the conclusion of the argument I just gave was that even while in e_1, I should choose to smoke. So, that argument "proved" something that is never in fact justified by any evidence I ever *actually* have. Most counterexamples to an argument proceed by showing that the premises of the argument can be true when the conclusion is false. This counterexample proceeds by showing that the premises of the argument I gave can be fully justified when the conclusion never is justified. So I suppose once again I should not say that I have shown an argument "invalid." Let's say I have shown it "nearly invalid." Since we must reject the argument I gave, we also must reject clause (1) of Principle B. To the extent that people really are talking about clause (1) of Principle B when they speak of "the weak dominance principle," the weak dominance principle is an unacceptable principle of rational choice. I believe the implausibility of Principle B should have been clear from my analysis of the Allais gambles and the Ellsberg gambles, but as you say, Casey, more people will accept the plausibility of Policy C, my Carnapian rule for picking reference classes, than will accept the cogency of my certainty policy or my real propensity policy.

CASEY: You have me convinced by this objection to clause (1) of Principle B, Jack. And I admit you have made me a bit suspicious of clause (2) as well. That, of course, is the clause that is operative in Simpson's Paradox, as it was formulated in that magazine article you read, although I suppose one could call the "nearly invalid" argument you gave a version of Simpson's Paradox, too. Clause (2) of Principle B—the "strong dominance" clause—is the principle of inference of some arguments you and I both agree are compelling, for example, the Businessman Argument. Do you have a similar counterexample to clause (2) of Principle B?
JACK: No.

Notes

1. L. J. Savage, *The Foundations of Statistics*. 2nd ed. (New York: Dover), 6.

2. Savage, *Foundations of Statistics*, 21.

3. Savage tried hard to write down a version of STP that does not make reference to knowledge. It is worth asking whether he gave good reasons for this effort, and it is worth asking whether he succeeded. I will not explore either of these questions.

4. I thank Eldar Shafir for this example.

5. Lest one suffer "the experimenter effect." See "Savage's Thought Experiment" later in this chapter.

6. I do not mean to imply that the Businessman Argument is a rare example of a persuasive QCD. They are common. For instance, Friedman and Savage give this example: "Suppose a physician now knows that his patient has one of several diseases for each of which the physician would prescribe immediate bed rest. We assert that under this circumstance the physician should and, unless confused, will prescribe immediate bed rest." M. Friedman and L. J. Savage, "The Expected-Utility Hypothesis and the Measurability of Utility," *Journal of Political Economy* 60 (1952): 468, cited in E. F. McClennen, *Rationality and Dynamic Choice: Foundational Explorations* (Cambridge: Cambridge University Press, 1990), 48. This example suggests, probably accurately, that QCDs, and plausible ones, occur frequently in medical decision-making.

7. The earliest such experiments are due to Maurice Allais and Daniel Ellsberg. Maurice Allais, "The Foundations of a Positive Theory of Choice Involving Risk and a Criticism of the American School," in *Expected Utility Hypotheses and the Allais Paradox*, ed. M. Allais and O. Hagen (Dordrecht, Boston: Reidel, 1979), 27–145. (The original article appeared, in French, in 1953.) Daniel Ellsberg, "Risk, Ambiguity, and the Savage Axioms," *Quarterly Journal of Economics* 75 (1961): 643–669. Also, importantly, there are the disjunction effect essays. A. Tversky and E. Shafir, "The Disjunction Effect in Choice under Uncertainty," *Psychological Science* 3 (1992): 305–309; E. Shafir and A. Tversky, "Thinking through Uncertainty: Non-consequential Reasoning and Choice," *Cognitive Psychology* 24 (1992): 449–474.

8. The Hawaii vacation experiment and sequential coin toss experiment are from Tversky and Shafir, "Disjunction Effect."

9. More than 60 percent of the subjects who were given the "Don't Know" problem chose to buy the right to wait in order to make their decision when the exam outcome was known. See Tversky and Shafir "Disjunction Effect," 305.

10. The actual results were as follows. In the condition where the subjects assumed that they won the first gamble, 69 percent of the subjects accepted the second gamble; 31 percent of the subjects rejected it. In the condition where the subjects assumed that they lost the first gamble, 59 percent of the subjects accepted

the second gamble; 41 percent of the subjects rejected the second gamble. In the condition where they did not know the result of the first gamble, 36 percent of the subjects accepted the second gamble; 64 percent of the subjects rejected the second gamble.

To estimate the reliability of choice, the basic gamble was presented to a comparable group of subjects twice several weeks apart, and only 19 percent of the subjects made different decisions on the two occasions. These results were replicated in a between-subjects design, and the distribution of choices was nearly identical to the choices in the within-subjects design, indicating that the subjects in the within-subjects design truly evaluated the choices independently.

11. For example, see Shafir and Tversky, "Disjunction Effect," 456.

12. Savage, *Foundations of Statistics*, 7.

13. The Allais Paradox was first presented by Maurice Allais in a series of three memoirs written for or immediately after the 1952 Paris International Colloquium on Risk Theory. The third of these, "Fondoments d'une Théorie Positive des Choix Comportant un Risque et Critique des Postulats et Axiomes de L'Ecole Americaine." was published in *Econométrie*, Colloques Internationaux du Centre National de la Recherche Scientifique 40 (Paris: 1953), 257–332. An English translation, "The Foundations of a Positive Theory of Choice Involving Risk and a Criticism of the Postulates and Axioms of the American School," appeared in Allais and Hagen, *Expected utility Hypotheses and the Allais Paradox: Contemporary Discussions of Decisions under Uncertainty with Allais' Rejoinder* (Dordrecht, Boston: Reidel, 1979), in which the experiment now referred to as the "Allais Paradox" appears on pp. 88–90.

The Allais experiment has since been corroborated by MacCrimmon, Moskowitz, and Slovic and Tversky: K. MacCrimmon, "An Experimental Study of the Decision Making Behavior of Business Executives," Ph.D. diss., University of California, Los Angeles, 1965; H. Moskowitz, "Effects of Problem Representation and Feedback on Rational Behavior in Allais and Morlat-Type Problems," *Decision Science* 5 (1974): 225–241; P. Slovic and A. Tversky, "Who Accepts Savage's Axiom?" *Behavioral Science* 19 (1974): 368–373.

14. Savage, *Foundations of Statistics*, 101. Savage's discussion of the Allais Problem is on pp. 101–103.

15. Savage, *Foundations of Statistics*, 103. I have changed the quotation slightly to fit with the labeling in table 1.1.

16. The wording of the sure-thing principle has been changed slightly from Savage, *Foundations of Statistics*, 21, to make clear that I intend it to be read prescriptively.

17. Savage does not make this argument. But it might be "intuitively obvious" to a theorist with his conception of the "correct" elements of structure for a decision problem.

18. W. Labov, "Empirical Foundations of Linguistic Theory," in *The Scope of American Linguistics*, ed. R. Austerlitz (Ghent: Peter De Ridder Press, 1975), 77–133.

19. This portrayal of Jack's reaction is consistent with the results of an experiment by P. Slovic and A. Tversky, "Who Accepts Savage's Axiom," in which subjects who had made a choice that would be recommended by Casey's reasoning were given Jack's original reasons, and subjects who made Jack's original choices were given Casey's reasoning. More subjects switched from a "Casey choice" to a "Jack choice" than vice versa.

20. There are experimental results that show that people are more willing to bet on coin tosses that have not been made than on tosses that have been made, although which side of the coin turned up has not yet been revealed. E. Langer, "The Illusion of Control," *Journal of Personality and Social Psychology* 32 (1975): 311–328. And there are analogous results not involving coins in Shafir and Tversky, "Disjunction Effect." A good theory of what is going on in these experiments might show that my simple description of "epistemic states" is too simple.

21. An aside on terminology: Even before Jack knows the result of the lottery, it is possible for him to reason about "the result of the lottery," or "the winning ticket." For instance, he can say that the result of the lottery may make someone very happy. It is not necessary to interpret Jack here as unknowingly referring to a lottery ticket with a particular number (or to the event of a given ticket being chosen) to make sense of his statement. Rather, we can use the expression "the result of the lottery" to stand in for whatever ticket-number might (epistemically) turn out to win.

George Wilson has argued that definite descriptions sometimes play essentially the same grammatical role as "parameters" (in R Thomason's terminology) in a Fitch-style natural deduction system. For example, the existential generalization "(Ex)(Fx)" might be instantiated by the sentence "Fa," where "a" is a parameter. A person who makes this step of inference does not have some particular object in mind that she is calling "a." Parameters are not singular referring terms. Similarly, since Jack and Casey know *there will be* a result of the lottery, they can use the definite description "the result of the lottery" in a parameter-like way. George Wilson, "Pronouns and Pronominal Descriptions: A New Semantical Category," *Philosophical Studies* 45 (1984): 1–30. I am indebted to Mark Wilson for suggesting this treatment of definite descriptions like "the result of the lottery" in the presence of a several epistemic alternatives, or possibilities.

22. Edward Tufte, *Visual Explanations* (Cheshire, Conn. Graphics Press, 1997), 23–24.

23. It is not easy to think up short, clear, and real examples of the damage done to communication when Principle G★ (or G) fails. For instance, in the ordinary case of a person who lies, even a person who lies a great deal, it is not the validity of the person's inferences that is in question, though the truth of her premises may be. And even when some of the person's inferences cannot be trusted to be valid, the damage done to

communication often is minimized because other, trustworthy, patterns of inference "take up the slack." This does not happen in the NASA case, because the NASA officials have such a limited repertoire of effective communication with laypersons.

24. Running, as everyone knows, in the Seventh at Aqueduct. See *A Fugue for Tin Horns*.

25. Later I will consider the suggestion that arguments like Casey's (or Savage's) are special cases of backtracking reasoning, special cases in which the backtracking criticism is also a cogent criticism of the rationality of a decision at the time it is made. For now, I shall ignore this possible maneuver.

26. When Jack understands (4) as (4R), and (2) as (2 K), in order to interpret the subargument as valid he will need to understand (3) in a compatible way, as follows. (3 K) Since G1 and G2 have the same payoff, $500,000, for the results in the set R_{12-100}, if *I know* that the ticket that is chosen belongs to the set of results R_{12-100}, *I also know* that if I were to choose G2 I would get the same payoff ($500,000) that I would get from choosing G1, and since G3 and G4 have the same payoff, $0, for the results in the set R_{12-100}, if *I know* that the ticket that is chosen belongs to the set of results R_{12-100}, *I also know* that if I were to choose G3, I would get the same payoff ($0) that I would get from choosing G4.

This, together with (2 K), would be a good argument for (4) understood as (4R), that is, as a criticism of the rationality of Jack's decision. (3 K) obviously is true, so if Jack *knew* that the ticket that is chosen belongs to the set 12–100, then he would also know that he would actually get the same payoff from G1 that he would get from G2, and that he would actually get the same payoff from G3 as he would get from G4.

27. Essentially this objection to representing the Allais problem in lottery format has been given by others. Peter C. Fishburn remarks that "as Allais originally argued and has insistently maintained, [the lottery version] is inadmissible as a guide to rationality since it destroys the holistic natures of the prospects under consideration." Fishburn generally agrees. Jack's ultimate aim is to defend the reasonableness of what he will call "ellsbergian policies." He is not *merely* trying to refute sure-thing reasoning. This will emerge more clearly later. See Peter C. Fishburn, *Nonlinear Preference and Utility Theory* (Baltimore: Johns Hopkins University Press, 1988), 38–39.

28. See the experiments cited in note 13.

29. This "factoring in" strategy is Paul Samuelson's way of dealing with goods that accrue to an agent as a result of merely taking a bet: "Probability, Utility and the Independence Axiom," *Econometrica* 20 (1952): 670–678.

30. In a nutshell, losses seem worse to people who are happy. See, for instance, A. Isen, T. Nygren, and F. Ashby, "Influence of Positive Affect on the Subjective Utility of Gains and Losses: It Is Just Not Worth the Risk," *Journal of Personality and Social Psychology* 55 (1988): 710–717.

31. Hilary Putnam is unwilling to make this move. See Hilary Putnam, "Rationality in Decision Theory and in Ethics," *Critica* 18, 54 (1986): 3–16.

32. See "The Lawyer Argument" earlier in this chapter.

33. Like the pair of choices G1 over G2 and G4 over G3 in the Allais Problem, Jack's pair of choices here violates the principle of expected utility maximization. The reasoning to show this is similar to the reasoning in the Allais case, and I will skip it here.

34. I am indebted to Brian Hill for helpful discussions of this line of thought.

35. Ellsberg, "Risk, Ambiguity, and the Savage Axioms," *Quarterly Journal of Economics* 75 (1961): 643–669.

36. Ellsberg, "Risk, Ambiguity, and the Savage Axioms," 659–660.

37. Slovic and Tversky, "Who Accepts Savage's Axiom." Kenneth MacCrimmon and Stig Larsson, "Utility Theory: Axioms versus 'Paradoxes'," in Allais and Hagen, *Expected Utility Hypotheses*, 333–409. A helpful review of more recent literature can be found in C. Camerer and M. Weber, "Recent Developments in Modeling Preferences: Uncertainty and Ambiguity," *Journal of Risk and Uncertainty* 5 (1992): 325–370.

38. In connection with Jack's real propensity policy, it is interesting to note that experiments show that people prefer to take bets when they have reason to believe that at the time they make the bet they have all the information they believe there is to be had about the random device that will determine the payoff. For instance, most people prefer to bet on a coin that is still in the air to betting on one that has already landed, even if they have no particular reason to believe that their opponent knows which side landed up. There has been some speculation that this is due to so-called quasi-magical thinking; that is, people act as if they believe that if they bet while the coin is in the air they will be able to influence how it falls, something that could not be the case after it has fallen. See Shafir and Tversky, "Disjunction Effect." I am inclined to think Jack's line of thought is more plausible. While the coin is still in the air, the bettor has all the information anyone could have about the relevant physical properties of the coin, including that it has a 0.5 propensity to fall heads-up (stipulating that it is known to be a fair coin). After it has fallen, though, there is a crucial physical property the bettor does not know—which side is up. One of Jack's reasons for adopting the real propensity policy was that when there is relevant information "out there" that the agent lacks, she is at greater risk than when there is no such information. She is at risk even when she has no positive reason to think others possess the relevant information she lacks. (Thanks again to Brian Hill for helpful discussions of this matter).

39. Thanks to Hartry Field for showing me a "gene X" form of Simpson's Paradox.

40. Jack is following W. Salmon's discussion of these matters in W. Salmon, "Statistical Explanation," in *Statistical Explanation and Statistical Relevance*, ed. W. Salmon (Pittsburgh: University of Pittsburgh Press, 1971), 29–87.

MAKING RATIONAL CHOICES
WHEN PREFERENCES CYCLE

I will start by describing a familiar normative theory of rational choice—a theory that aims to specify the most rational choice for an agent to make in a sense of 'rational' that does not quite mean "rational." I will start describing the theory by describing its ontology, and some idealizations that shape that ontology.

Assume X is a set of outcomes of interest to a certain agent. X might include "get a cheese sandwich," "get a bowl of chili," "stay dry," "get wet," "go out carrying your umbrella," "go out having left your umbrella at home." Call the outcomes in this set x, y, z, x_1, y_1, and so on. We can define a set P of probability measures on X. Each measure p in P assigns some probability or other (perhaps zero or one) to some outcomes in X. For each measure, the probabilities must add to one (by the definition of "probability measure").[1] For example, p might be {0.5 get wet, 0.5 stay dry}. These probability measures are to be understood as representing the probabilities of outcomes consequent upon performing some action. Perhaps if you go out leaving your umbrella at home, you confront the probabilities {0.5 get wet, 0.5 stay dry}. Perhaps if you go to the cafeteria and buy whatever they have left, you confront the probabilities {0.8 get a cheese sandwich, 0.2 get a bowl of chili}, since people mainly avoid the cheese sandwiches. So, in this ontology, possible actions are represented by a "spread" of probabilities over possible outcomes. Actions *are* what they are likely to bring about.

In the set P of probability measures, there will be "one-point" measures, assigning probability 1 (certainty) to some outcome. Example: the measure {1.0 get a cheese sandwich}, that is, the measure that assigns absolute certainty to getting a cheese sandwich—in this ontology, the possible action of getting a cheese sandwich for sure. We identify this with the outcome itself, "get a cheese sandwich." The outcome set X thus has an image in the probability, or possible action, set P. In general, we identify the probability measure p, which assigns probability 1.0 to outcome x, with outcome x. We call this measure $x^\star$, just to keep track. This is a metaphysical move made for epistemological purposes. Our epistemological motivation is that by making these identifications, we are able to *interpret* a powerful mathematical theorem as expressing the basic relationships of expected utility theory.

The foregoing probabilities are *subjective* probabilities. They reflect the agent's degree of confidence that a given outcome will ensue, consequent upon her performing a given action. More generally, they reflect the agent's degree of confidence that a given event will occur (or has occurred, or is occurring). This brings us to the first of several prescriptions laid down by this theory: An agent must modify her degrees of confidence so that they are expressible by probability measures. That is, she must modify her degrees of confidence so that they obey the usual axioms of the probability calculus (if they already do so, then she must leave them alone). This theory is Cartesian rather than Spinozistic, in that it assumes that an agent's degrees of confidence (essentially, her beliefs or "degrees of belief") are within her power to adjust. Much experimental evidence shows that the degrees of confidence humans attach to various outcomes do *not* obey the probability calculus. Much of this same evidence suggests that the agent cannot do very much to alter the misfit.[2] But that will not be the problem addressed in this essay. The problem addressed in this essay has to do with a similar "misfit" that sometimes exists between an agent's *preferences among outcomes* and some further requirements laid down by the theory I am considering.

The theory assumes that an agent has preferences among the possible actions available to her at a given time. Indeed, the theory prescribes something even stronger than that the agent have some preferences and some indifferences. When she does not prefer action p to action q, and she does not prefer q to p either, she is said to be indifferent between p and q. If we write "p Pref q" for "the agent prefers p to q," and we write "*p* Ind *q*" for "the agent is indifferent between *p* and *q*," then the theory prescribes that for all possible actions "seriously" confronting the agent, either *p* Pref *q*, or *q* Pref *p*, or *p* Ind *q*. It will come as no surprise that philosophers can differ over which possible actions "seriously confront" an agent at a given time. Suppose at some later time the agent's deepest personal values change, and as a result she contemplates courses of action she never before even considered (going on a hunger strike, running for Congress). At the earlier time, these are in some sense "possible actions" for the agent, although even contemplating doing one of them never played a role in her life. Do these possible actions belong in *P*? That, too, is an important philosophical problem that lies outside the bounds of this discussion.

To get at the problem I do want to discuss here, we must look at further requirements the theory imposes on an agent's preferences (and indifferences). In the Von Neumann–Morgenstern "tradition"—one of several traditional ways to articulate what is essentially the same theory— three special requirements are imposed on an agent's preferences and indifferences. The agent must see to it that her preferences and indifferences conform to these requirements, just as she must see to it that her degrees of confidence satisfy the axioms of the probability calculus. Let us think of these requirements imposed on the agent's preferences and in-differences as "axioms" of the theory, and call them A_1, A_2, and A_3 (presented in full in note 3).[3]

Once an agent has conformed her preferences (and indifferences— from now on I will just say "preferences") to A_1, A_2, and A_3, a theorem can be proved about the agent, with the following main clauses.

(a) There is a function *u* mapping possible actions (probability measures) in *P* into the real numbers, and this function *u* has the property:

$$u(p) > u(q) \text{ if and only if } p \text{ Pref } q$$

(b) This property of *u* is preserved by linear transformations of scale, in the sense that when

$$0 \leq r \leq 1, \ u(rp + (1 - r)q) = ru(p) + (1 - r)u(q).$$

(c) Suppose we define *u* on *X* (the set of outcomes) by: $u(x) = u(x\star)$. Then,

$$u(p) = \Sigma u(x)p(x).$$

The right side of this last equation is just the usual formula for the expected utility of a possible action p.

Now suppose an agent is contemplating a certain set of possible actions, and one of these actions (say, p) is such that $u(p)$ is larger than $u(q)$ for any other action q in the set. By clause (a) of the theorem, we have it that p Pref q for each alternative q. The sense of 'rational' invoked by this theory is that it is rational for the agent to do what she most prefers doing. So the theory obliges the agent to perform p. If there is a tie for highest u-value, the theory is silent on how the tie should be broken, though proponents of the theory often recommend randomizing in such cases.

Taking clauses (a), (b), and (c) of the theorem together, the function u seems a very good candidate to be called the agent's "utility" function. It puts a (thoroughly subjective) value on both outcomes and possible actions in such a way that higher value means "preferred to." Moreover, utilities of outcomes, and probabilities that these outcomes will be realized if one does such-and-such, can be combined in the usual way for computing "values"—expected utilities—of possible actions. The "u value" of a possible action is just its expected utility, though this idea has appeared as an end-product of reasoning, rather than as a starting point. The importance of this is that there are long-run convergence theorems, such as the laws of large numbers and the central limit theorems, that may be thought to show that it must be wisest to act always so as to maximize expected utility. Our theorem maps the terrain in a way that enables us to identify a plausible candidate for "expected utility," so we can help ourselves to these convergence theorems if we wish. Whether it *is* philosophically helpful to do so is another matter beyond the scope of this discussion.

Many writers have taken the view that the requirements imposed by A_1, A_2, and A_3 have "nearly" the status of laws of logic. Here, for example, is Bryan Skyrms, discussing Frank Ramsey's somewhat different set of "first principles" for an essentially similar theory:

> These are the key ideas of the procedure by which Ramsey extracted from a rich and coherent preference ordering over gambles both a subjective utility and a subjective degree of belief such that the preference ordering agrees with the ordering by magnitude of expected utility. Utility has now shed the psychological and moral associations with which it was associated in the eighteenth and nineteenth centuries.

The theory of expected utility is now a part of *logic*: the logic of coherent preference. (Emphasis in the original)[4]

Now it may be that Skyrms wishes to draw a line around the part of the theory he calls "the theory of expected utility" in such a way that this theory is understood to contain only the representation theorem, which is, of course, necessarily true. But I think he means the full doctrine I have just described, or a closely similar doctrine. Skyrms is not alone in this opinion, and it may be the majority opinion among proponents of the theory.

I do not wish to discuss A_2 or A_3. I will concentrate on A_1, the "weak order axiom." Indeed, I will concentrate on just one implication of A_1: the implication that an agent must not have a set of preferences of the form $\{p_1 \text{ Pref } p_2, p_2 \text{ Pref } p_3, \ldots, p_n \text{ Pref } p_1\}$.

Such a set of preferences is said to constitute a "cycle." Cyclic preferences are not transitive. An agent's preferences can fail to be transitive when they do not cycle—for example, when for some p, q, and r, p Pref q and q Pref r, but p Ind r.

2

Proponents of subjective expected utility theory often speak as though an agent who allowed some of her preferences to cycle would be as irrational as a person who allowed some of her beliefs to form an obviously inconsistent set. Perhaps this would be Skyrms's view; it seems a reasonable inference from his assimilation of the principles of expected utility theory to laws of logic. Now, it may be that it is always better not to have cyclic preferences. But this is not because to do so is to make an error tantamount to an error of simple logic. The argument that cyclic preferences are rationally acceptable rests, ultimately, on the availability of a utility theory that seems quite reasonable, but that tolerates preference cycles. Since this nonstandard utility theory seems not to be widely known among philosophers who do not specialize in decision theory, my aim in this essay will be the modest one of showing how this nonstandard utility theory works in practice, and providing some general philosophical background and commentary. As is the case with Von Neumann–Morgenstern utility theory, the harder part of developing this nonstandard theory has been mathematical, not philosophical, and has been done by others.

First, some background on "multivariate" decision-making: that is, decision-making when the agent must compare possible actions on several different dimensions of evaluation. Here is an example based loosely on the literature on medical decision-making. In this case, the agent is faced with a personal decision, the type where decision theory is supposed to be of use. Sarah is ill, and her doctor tells her that unless she is treated she has only three months to live. Her doctor also tells her that medical procedures are available to her that differ from each other along two dimensions—the number of years of life they offer and the risk that she will die during the procedure.[5] Suppose that before being confronted with any particular alternatives, Sarah does some preliminary thinking, guided by an article on medical decision-making her doctor has given her. She thinks carefully about what things she values, and why she values them. She talks with friends and family about what they see her values as being. By this combination of introspection and considering the picture others have of her, she decides what tradeoffs among the relevant variables she is prepared to make. The following is her analysis.

Life expectancy is more important than risk of death from the procedure if this risk is fairly low, say no higher than 15 percent. Consideration of life expectancy should be the controlling factor as far as possible. But a difference of a year or less in life expectancy means very little for life expectancies of around two years or longer. Such (relatively) small gains in life expectancy are not worth a modest increase in risk, say 5 percent or more. The more she reflects on this conception, the clearer she is that it is exactly what she thinks and feels, and the more committed to it she becomes. She decides that she will figure out as much as possible about the relative desirability of various procedures by comparing the life expectancies they offer, with the provisos mentioned, and only move to comparisons of risk if necessary to complete the picture. She is glad she read the article on decision theory. She asks her doctor for the specific details of the available procedures.

These details could not be more galling. Three procedures are possible, and for each, very solid statistical evidence about risk and long-term survival is available. The evidence is summarized in table 2.1.

Sarah starts by looking only at the life expectancy column, as her policy requires. This enables her to decide that she prefers procedure C to procedure A. The difference in life expectancy is substantial, and this is the first factor she has decided to take into account, moving to morbidity-risk differences only if life expectancy considerations do not settle the matter.

TABLE 2.1.   What Sarah learns about the three
medical procedures.

Procedure	Life expectancy	Morbidity for procedure
A	2 years	5%
B	3 years	10%
C	4 years	15%

But the one-year differences in life expectancy between A and B, and between B and C, are matched with 5 percent differences in risk. These increments in life expectancy are too (relatively) small to settle the matter without looking to increments in risk. So that is what she does. When she goes to the risk column, she determines that A is preferable to B and B preferable to C. If she were to rank A and C by looking at the risk column, she would rank A preferable to C, but she has been able to rank A and C in terms of life expectancy, so she disregards the comparison of A and C on her "secondary" dimension of risk. So be it. This set of preferences reflects her best diagnosis and articulation of her most important relevant values. Her preferences are: A preferred to B, B preferred to C, and C preferred to A; a cycle.

Sarah has reasoned her way to these preferences by applying principles of choice that have a firm basis in carefully examined values. But, she has no most-preferred, or coequally most-preferred, choice. This is tragic, clearly. But is it irrational? Proponents of subjective expected utility theory usually argue that anyone who, like Sarah, has cyclic preferences can be turned into a "money pump" for some sort of value (perhaps not money). Then it is claimed that it is deeply irrational to accept being a money pump.

The argument that a person with cyclic preferences will of necessity become a money pump goes like this. Suppose someone has the following cycle of preferences. She prefers A to B, she prefers B to C, and she prefers C to A. Suppose she presently has C in her possession. Since she prefers B to C, she will (should) be willing to pay something in order to be able to trade C for B. And since she prefers A to B, she will be willing to pay something in order to trade B for A. And since she prefers C to A, she will be willing to pay something to trade A for C. But now she has C again, and the sequence of "purchased" exchanges will begin again, or at least ought to begin again, given her preferences. She will cycle again and again through these trades, losing money (or some other thing of value) at every step, until she is broke (or until she has squandered her entire supply of the non-monetary thing of value). Even if the person does not make these trades, her preferences rationally require her to do so. Her preferences rationally require that she act so as to ruin herself. This, it is held, is *practically* irrational.

But Sarah does not end up being a money pump. Here is why. She has been studying her copy of the article on medical decision-making, and has learned that even in these tragic circumstances, she must make some decision or other; she must choose one procedure or another rather than choosing none. And her decision must be a reasoned decision. Finally, the choice procedure she employs must be as compatible as possible with her examined values, tragically configured though they may be. The article recommends that in situations of the kind she finds herself in, the agent might consider deciding on the basis of the most important dimension only. Sarah thinks about that, and decides it is the procedure to use. So she chooses procedure C.

This rule of choice does not turn her into a money pump. She would not accept the sequence of exchanges that would, ultimately, fritter away all her goods. That sequence of exchanges is not dictated by her choice rule.

And this is not an arbitrary, obstinate refusal; it is reasoned. (1) She prefers deciding to not deciding, but (2) she cannot decide by picking a (possibly coequally) most preferred option, so (3) she decides by reverting to a rule that has some but not all elements in common with the rule she appealed to when she articulated her preferences among procedures. Sarah acts on several of her preferences among various things, but she does not act on her preferences among medical procedures themselves. These she holds constant, cycling.

Sarah will be distressed by her choice, and might need counseling. In part this can be explained by the fact that she has not been able to act on her preferences among medical procedures, preferences that rest on deeply held values. She has acted on her values to an extent, but not fully, and they are important values affecting a monumental personal decision. This shows that it would be a mistake to think her preferences merely changed when she finally worked out a way to decide, and acted on it. Preferences are not always "revealed in action," as a common slogan of that kind of behaviorism would have it.

A proponent of standard subjective expected utility theory might reply that although Sarah has indeed acted on her favorite decision rule, this does not keep her from being a money pump. Her preferences among medical procedures cycle, and that is that. She is rationally obliged to pay a "fee" for the right to "trade up" (or "around") her preference ranking, whatever she does in fact. Therefore, she is tolerating preferences that rationally require her to ruin herself. Therefore, she is irrational.

This claim is based on one, or both, of the following two assumptions.

First assumption: Sarah's utility for A is higher than her utility for B, for example, since she prefers A to B. That is why, if she has B, she is rationally required to throw in something valuable, something that makes up the utility difference, if she trades B for A.[6] Thus the money pump.

But Sarah does not have utilities for medical procedures. Since her preferences violate the weak order axiom, she does not satisfy a precondition of the theory. For Sarah, there is no real-valued function u such that when Sarah prefers p to q, $u(p) > u(q)$.

Second assumption: Utilities aside, since Sarah prefers A to B, there simply *must* be some amount of "money" she is willing to pay out, along with B, to get A.

One suspects that this second assumption covertly rests on the first assumption—what is preferred "simply must" have greater *value*. But let us approach the second assumption from a different angle, and examine the scare quotation marks around "money."

No universal kind of subjective value, called "utility," is attached to A, B, or C for Sarah. We are no longer operating with the metaphysics of the standard theory. So "money" must mean money, or parcels of real estate, or fun in the sun, or some other thing that is real and really has value. So the claim made in the second assumption must be this. There is some real thing, or perhaps there are notes or IOUs written in terms of a specified wide range of such real things, and Sarah is rationally required (for instance) to exchange B plus some quantity of these real things (or notes for them) to obtain A.

But people say there are some things money cannot buy. Taken as a psychological claim about people, common sense grants that this is right. The sexist jibe that every woman has her price is false, and it is false regardless of what currency one considers (even, as some accounts relate, the currency of relief from torture, though in that currency probably a great many people do have a price). Consumer research shows that it is common for people to keep separate "accounts," psychologically, for value of different kinds, such as value that tends to be acquired and lost in different environments, value "targeted" for particular exchanges, or value associated with different activities in life.[7] Sometimes the boundaries between these "accounts" cannot be crossed, in the sense that the person will not draw down on one account to refurbish another, although she may draw down on it to achieve some other well-defined end. There are things that money of one "kind" cannot buy, but money of another kind can.[8]

If evidence exists, other than the assumptions of traditional economists, to show that despite all this, there is some real thing of value that real people are willing to treat as a universal currency, I am unaware of it. If there is, perhaps one could argue that Sarah should be willing to keep paying a fee in this universal currency in order to trade "up her preference ranking" among medical procedures, thereby becoming a "universal-currency pump." Perhaps one could even argue that Sarah should be willing to treat something as such a universal currency, regardless of her psychological dispositions to the contrary, just so she can go and make these ruinous trades. But until someone provides these preliminary arguments, we need not accept this form of the money pump argument, which rests on the claim that a person with cyclic preferences is rationally required to make money-pump exchanges.

One can mean other things by "money-pump argument." For instance, one can mean that the very rationale a person has for making choices is bound to result in the person being a money pump. This is the meaning I gave it when I said Sarah would *not* be a money pump because she has a coherent choice policy that does not dictate money-pump exchanges. When one says a person will be a money pump, one can also mean that the person will be psychologically compelled to accept money-pump exchanges if she acts as she wishes. It does not seem that this is true of Sarah.

Here is another criticism of Sarah's decision procedure. Since Sarah does not have utilities for the three medical procedures A, B, and C, she has deprived herself of expected utility reasoning without replacing it with a decision rule of comparable generality. The decision rule she has adopted to decide what medical procedure to have is far from general. How one might extend it to a wide range of cases is far from obvious, even though the "general advice" on making important decisions she read in the article was reasonable.

This seems right. But it is not clear how strong an objection it is. Is making a choice by means of a principle of decision that is not as general as standard utility theory sufficient for being irrational in a way, or to a degree, that approaches the irrationality of allowing one's beliefs to violate simple logic? I think that would be a hard case to make. Nevertheless, perhaps we have here some sort of interesting criticism of Sarah's rationality. Let us assume so, and move on to another possible criticism of her rationality.

The criticism is this: Sarah's method of choice requires that she ignore the morbidity risk of the three medical procedures in order to make some choice or other, consistent with some of her important values. But morbidity risk is important to her as well, even though it is of secondary importance when compared with life expectancy. It is a serious drawback of a decision-making policy that it sometimes requires us to ignore certain aspects of the possible actions we are considering, when those aspects play an important role in our evaluation of the actions. In the sphere of practical reason, it is as irrational to do that as it would be to ignore relevant evidence in the sphere of theoretical reason.

Granted that this is a flaw in Sarah's decision-making policy, is it enough of a flaw to render her "irrational"? The answer to this question is not clear-cut. On the one hand, Sarah has a very good reason for ignoring some factors that matter to her. This seems to speak for her rationality. On the other hand, if she had a policy that enabled her to take into account every factor that was important to her, surely that policy would be more rational than the one she uses. Consider the analogy with belief once more. Suppose someone has to form one belief or another right away, despite the fact that she is still in possession of inconsistent evidence. Under these conditions, a policy that allowed the person to form a belief, rather than leaving her suspended between several competing beliefs, would be desirable, even if the policy worked by specifying which evidence to ignore. Nevertheless, a belief-forming policy that enabled the person to take all of her relevant evidence into account would be more desirable, more rational. Perhaps we should say that Sarah is less than fully rational, and that this is one reason her circumstances are tragic.

In order to show how someone with cyclic preferences can make a choice according to a decision rule that is "fully rational," I will switch to a different hypothetical case. The agent in this example also has cyclic preferences, and, moreover (like Sarah), has good reason to allow her preferences to cycle. But the agent in this hypothetical example uses a decision-making rule that (a) is comparable to standard subjective expected utility theory in its generality, and (b) allows her to take into account all the dimensions of a "multidimensional" evaluation of alternative possible actions.

3

Susan is a 14-year-old girl who has three boyfriends, Tom, Bob, and Bill. In summary, their salient characteristics in Susan's eyes are as shown in table 2.2.

When Susan compares these boys as prospective dates, she prefers Tom to Bob, and Bob to Bill, but Bill to Tom. She has arrived at these preferences thoughtfully. She does not value any one of the "salient characteristics" more than any other, so she could not apply a Sarah-like rule even if she wanted to. She notes that Tom is better than Bob on two of the criteria, Bob is better than Bill on two, and Bill is better than Tom on two. So her preferences cycle: She prefers dating Tom to dating Bob, she prefers dating Bob to dating Bill, and she prefers dating Bill to dating Tom.

Sometimes this cycle is irrelevant. Not all the boys ask Susan for a date on every possible occasion. If only one does, she has no problem. If exactly two do, she always has a most preferred choice. But sometimes all three ask her out at the same time. Some girls would be daunted, and might even be money pumps because of it. Fortunately for Susan, she mastered decision theory for an eighth-grade project, and she sees how to solve her problem. Here is how she thinks it through.

The set X of relevant outcomes consists of the events being on a date with Tom, being on a date with Bob, and being on a date with Bill. Call these

TABLE 2.2.   The characteristics of Susan's boyfriends that lead to a preference cycle.

	Intelligence	Looks	Material possessions
Tom	Very smart	All right	Some nice stuff
Bob	Smart	Really good-looking	Not much nice stuff
Bill	Average	Pretty good-looking	Rich—nice car, beach house

x, y, and z. Susan's problem is how to decide among the possible actions $x^\star$, $y^\star$, and $z^\star$; that is, dating just Tom, dating just Bob, and dating just Bill. We have x Pref y, y Pref z, and z Pref x, and also $x^\star$ Pref $y^\star$, $y^\star$ Pref $z^\star$, and $z^\star$ Pref $x^\star$. No possible action is most preferred, nor is there a set of coequally most preferred possible actions. As a result, axiom A_1 of subjective expected utility theory—the "weak order" axiom—is violated, and Susan cannot make expected utility comparisons among $x^\star$, $y^\star$, and $z^\star$.

Fortunately, Susan knows about an alternative to the Von Neumann–Morgenstern utility theory, an alternative that does not not require that an agent's preferences obey the weak order constraint. Remember that the one-point measures $x^\star$, $y^\star$, and $z^\star$ are not the only probability measures in P. In addition, there are all the convex combinations $ax^\star + by^\star + cz^\star$, where a, b, and c are real numbers greater than or equal to zero, and such that a, b, and c add to one. Consider, for instance, the measure $1/3x^\star + 1/3y^\star + 1/3z^\star$. Suppose Susan thinks that if she goes to the Dairy Queen it is equally likely that she will run into one of Tom or Bob or Bill before she runs into any of the others. She might consider the possible action one would describe in English as "dating the first boy she runs into at the Dairy Queen." This possible action is expressible in the limited vocabulary of utility theory by the measure $1/3x^\star + 1/3y^\star + 1/3z^\star$. Susan can perform this possible action by going to the Dairy Queen. But suppose she does not want to be bothered going to the Dairy Queen. Then she can make a spinner in shop class, cover one-third of its surface with red paper, one-third with green paper, and one-third with blue paper. She can let red code "dating Tom," green code "dating Bob," and blue code "dating Bill." Then she can spin the spinner, and consider the possible action that would be described in English as "dating the boy whose color comes up on the spinner." Once again, in the ontology of utility theory, this is $1/3x^\star + 1/3y^\star + 1/3z^\star$. Call actions of this kind "spinner acts." Susan performs a spinner act by making the appropriate spinner, spinning it, and following through by doing what is indicated by the color on which the spinner stops. In fact, she would not want to perform the one-third, one-third, one-third spinner act, because she has no guarantee that there isn't some other act she should, rationally, prefer to it. But the general idea is helpful to her.

Susan knows that there are a number of theories of rational choice that are as general in their application as the standard theory (that is, they are subject-matter insensitive) but that differ from the standard theory by placing different sets of constraints on an agent. One of these theories is SSB utility theory. SSB utility theory is tailored for situations in which Pref exhibits cycles over the set of possible outcomes.

SSB utility theory does not employ a one-place utility functional u (a "functional" is a function that maps its domain into the real numbers). SSB utility theory employs a two-place "utility functional" f defined on $(P) \mathbf{X} (P)$. That is, f maps ordered pairs of possible actions (as usual, idealized as probability measures), including ordered pairs of "convex combinations" of such measures, into the reals. Definition of "convex combination of probability measures": If $p_1, p_2, \ldots, p_n$ are probability measures, and $a_1, a_2, \ldots, a_n$ are real numbers $0 \le a_i \le 1$ adding to one, then:

$$a_1 p_1 + a_2 p_2 + \cdots + a_n p_n$$

is a convex combination of $p_1, p_2, \ldots, p_n$.

Since the set X of outcomes has an image in P defined as usual by $x = x^\star$ ($x^\star$ being the measure assigning one—or "certainty"—to the outcome x), an SSB functional f also maps ordered pairs of outcomes, and convex combinations thereof, into the reals.

The idea of this theory is to have a mathematical guarantee that p Pref q exactly when $f(p,q) > 0$.[9] One can prove a theorem about SSB utility theory that goes as follows. A person's preferences satisfy a certain set of conditions if and only if there is an SSB functional f such that

$$p \text{ Pref } q \text{ if and only if } f(p, q) > 0$$

(and any other SSB functional $f^{\#}$ is such that p Pref q if and only if $f^{\#}(p, q) > 0$ is a positive multiple of f).

The "set of conditions" an agent must satisfy in order for this theorem to be applicable overlap to some extent with the analogous conditions for applicability of Von Neumann–Morgenstern utility theory. For example, the agent's degrees of confidence must obey the probability calculus. And the agent's preferences must obey certain "principles of coherence." But these principles are weaker than the corresponding principles of standard utility theory (axioms A_1, A_2, and A_3), and in fact are strictly implied by the standard axioms.[10] In particular, the SSB constraints on preference do not include weak order and do not imply it. In general, it is possible for Pref to exhibit cycles on outcomes and on possible actions, and still have the agent satisfy the requirements.

Susan sees to it that her degrees of confidence that various outcomes will follow upon performing various possible actions obey the laws of the probability calculus. And she sees to it that her preferences and indifferences obey the SSB axioms. This is a milder requirement than the requirement that one's preferences and indifferences obey axioms A_1, A_2, and A_3 of standard utility theory, but it still demands a higher degree of "coherence" in one's system of preferences than most people are likely to exhibit. Let us ignore that problem, though it is real and important. Once Susan has her degrees of confidence and her preferences "in order," her preferences are represented by an SSB functional f such that

$$p \text{ Pref } q \text{ if and only if } f(p, q) > 0.$$

Furthermore, Susan is concerned about a finite set of outcomes: dating Tom, dating Bob, and dating Bill. When the outcome set is finite, it can be shown that there is a nonempty set of possible actions such that no possible action is preferred to any member of that set. In order to compute what one of these possible actions is, Susan needs some psychological information about her preference structure. So she employs some standard psychological techniques to obtain enough information. She has already made use of these techniques to fine-tune her preferences and indifferences, so that they satisfy the requirements of SSB theory. She figures out that she is indifferent between (1) dating Tom and (2) a four-fifths chance of dating Bill plus a one-fifth chance of dating Bob. Moreover, she is indifferent between (1) dating Bob and (2) a one-half chance of dating Tom plus a one-half chance of dating Bill.[11] One can compute that in these circumstances, despite the cycle in her preferences over dating Tom, dating Bob, and dating Bill, there is a measure, a convex combination of dating Tom, dating Bob, and dating Bill, that is such that no other possible action is preferred to it. This measure is 4/9(date Tom) + 1/9(date Bob) + 4/9(date Bill). It corresponds to a spinner act. In order to perform it, Susan needs to build an appropriate spinner. She covers 4/9 of the surface of a spinner with red paper (for Tom), 1/9 of the surface with green paper (for Bob), and the remaining 4/9 of the surface with blue paper (for Bill). She spins her spinner and dates the lucky boy.[12] Her reasoning in choosing the spinner act is straightforward: "If I perform any of the actions 'date Tom,' 'date Bob,' or 'date Bill,' I will be performing an action I disprefer to some alternative. But if I perform the spinner act I have computed, this will not be so."

Unlike Sarah's, Susan's policy for making these decisions is completely general. It will not always yield a single action as the one such that she prefers nothing to it, just as standard utility theory sometimes yields a tie for highest expected utility. And, unlike Sarah, Susan's choice policy does take into account all of the dimensions on which she evaluates possible actions. But there is a problem about choosing to perform a spinner act, a problem that arises regardless of how the probabilities are cashed in. Spinner acts happen in distinguishable stages. First Susan spins the spinner, then she does what the spinner indicates she should do. In the hypothetical case I have been considering, after the spinner has stopped spinning, one or another of the three boys will be the indicated "winner." But whichever boy it is, Susan will prefer dating another boy. So, at *that* stage in her performance of the spinner act, how can it be rational of her to follow through and date the boy determined by the spinner?

This is an instance of a broader class of problems. Often, a suboptimal action can occur as a proper part of a "protracted" action that is optimal, and occur in such a way that if the suboptimal component action were replaced by a component action that, taken by itself, was preferable to the suboptimal action actually performed, then the protracted action would not be as desirable. Here are two examples.

1. A poker player finds herself holding what she is quite sure is a losing hand. But she plays it out anyway, in order to persuade the other players that she is a reckless or "loose" player. She knows this increases the likelihood that at some later stage of the game, some other players will stay in against her when in fact she holds the winning hand, as they might not do if they believed her to be a cautious, "tight" player who would not play out a hand unless it was very strong. This kind of sophisticated bluffing is practiced by all good poker players; the point of playing out the weak hand is to establish a helpful "reputation" in the game, not to win with the weak hand by scaring the other players into folding. But if one were to consider out of context the player's action of playing the bad hand, it clearly would be just that—playing out a bad hand. What matters to the player is optimizing her success at a protracted action—playing a few hours of poker—and she might be more successful at doing that if, once in a great while, she played a single hand badly, as though she overvalued it.

2. An agent applying standard subjective expected utility theory might find two or more possible actions in a tie for highest expected utility. Although the theory does not require it, the agent might elect to break the tie by randomizing—perhaps by tossing a coin if there is a two-way tie. But once the coin is tossed, and one of the actions "wins," one can ask why the agent should follow through and perform that action. After all, she should be indifferent between performing the action indicated by the outcome of the coin toss, and another possible action. This is not the same as Susan's situation, since the action indicated by the outcome of the coin toss is not dispreferred to any other action, but the issues seem essentially the same. Here the answer is that the agent has a choice policy that sometimes obliges her to perform protracted actions—though not as protracted as a long session of poker consisting of many hands. The agent sometimes is obliged to perform a protracted action consisting of a coin toss (or some other randomizing act) followed by performing the action indicated by the outcome of the random event. The agent's rationale for this policy is that she must do something rather than nothing, and making a random choice among expected-utility coequals is as good a technique as any.

Susan's situation is more like that of the poker player than like that of the expected utility maximizer. The expected utility maximizer need not randomize. She can just perform whichever of the tied actions she feels like performing. But the poker player has a special reason for including the action of playing out the bad hand as a component of the protracted action (playing the poker session) that she really cares about. That is how it is with Susan. Suppose Bill "wins" when she spins her spinner. Then unless she follows through and dates Bill, she has not performed the very spinner act she has calculated to be the only available possible action that is not dispreferred to anything.

In Susan's case, and in the case of the poker player, to argue that the person need not perform the suboptimal component act in a sequence of acts constituting a single protracted action is to commit the fallacy of division. It is to assume that an optimal whole (the protracted action) must be comprised of component acts that are themselves optimal taken singly, out of the context of the whole. The fallacy of division is easy to fall into when evaluative properties of composite wholes are at issue. It is no surprise that it is tempting here.

A few points remain to be made.

First, the reader may have wondered why it would not do as well for Susan to randomize, after the fashion of the standard expected utility theorist who confronts an expected-utility tie. Why should she not draw a name out of a hat into which she has put three pieces of paper, one saying "Tom," one saying "Bob," and one saying "Bill"? The answer is that this would be to perform the action $1/3x^\star + 1/3y^\star + 1/3z^\star$, and this "spinner act" is *not* such that no possible action is preferred to it. The action $4/9x^\star + 1/9y^\star + 4/9z^\star$ *is* such that no possible action is preferred to it.

Second, Susan will not be a money pump. Since no possible action is preferred to the spinner act she chooses, the sequence of money pump exchanges cannot get started. As Peter Fishburn has pointed out, the idea that someone in Susan's position has to be a money pump rests in part on the idea that all of her choices must be among $x^\star$, $y^\star$, and $z^\star$.[13] But in fact, convex combinations of $x^\star$, $y^\star$, and $z^\star$—spinner acts—are included among the available choices.

Third, there is a sense in which SSB utility theory falls short of being a fully general policy for decision-making. The sense is this. Standard expected utility theory will designate a most preferred, or coequally most preferred, possible action from *any* set of alternative possible actions (provided, of course, that the agent in question satisfies all of the theory's requirements). SSB utility theory will not do this. For example, Susan cannot find her correct choice just from the set $\{x^\star, y^\star, z^\star\}$. But the set of convex combinations of any set of possible actions is always available, so an agent who satisfies the requirements laid down by SSB utility theory always has some correct choice, but it may be a spinner act.[14]

It is true that we think of agents as contemplating alternative possible courses of action, and we think of theories of rational choice as aimed at showing us how to choose among these "preselected" alternatives. SSB utility theory was not able to help Susan do this. But it was able to help her get the same effect—in the end she had chosen a boy to date, and she could point to a sound theoretical basis for her choice policy.

Notes

1. Strictly: P is a nonempty convex set of probability measures defined on a Boolean algebra of subsets of X. The measures are simple (a simple measure assigns a probability to only finitely many points). All convex combinations likewise are simple. These details will not matter philosophically until later in this discussion.

They matter mathematically to the provability of the very strong Von Neumann–Morgenstern representation theorem, upon which several important philosophical claims in the next few pages rest.

2. A good example is what some researchers have called "scenario thinking." Often, when a person thinks through a plan of action, or considers the likely result of some process that has taken place or may take place, and the person does these things by contriving a story of how events may unfold, the person will judge the likelihood that events will unfold according to the scenario of the story as higher than the likelihood of at least one component event of the scenario. This always violates the laws of the probability calculus. See, for instance, A. Tversky and D. Kahneman, "Extensional versus Intuitive Reasoning: The Conjunction Fallacy in Probability Judgment," *Psychological Bulletin* 90 (1983): 293–315; R. Dawes, *Rational Choice in an Uncertain World* (New York: Harcourt, Brace, Jovanovich, 1988), 128–143; D. Kahneman and D. Lovallo, "Timid Decisions and Bold Forecasts: A Cognitive Perspective on Risk Taking," paper presented at the Conference on Fundamental Issues in Strategy, Silverado, Calif., 1990.

3. A_1 ("Weak Order"): Pref weakly orders P. To say that Pref is a weak order is to say that it is both asymmetric and negatively transitive. That is: p Pref $q =>$ not (q Pref p), and: not (p Pref q) and not (q Pref r) $=>$ not (p Pref r). A_1 implies that Pref, Ind, and either-Pref-or-Ind are transitive relations. A_1 also implies that p Ind q and q Pref $r => p$ Pref r. So, for instance, if an agent prefers sitting to walking and is indifferent between standing and sitting, then she prefers standing to walking.

A_2: ("Independence"): p Pref $q => [ap + (1 - a)r]$ Pref $[aq + (1 - a)r]$ for $0 < a < 1$, and for any measure r.

A_3: ("Continuity"): $[p$ Pref q and q Pref $r] => \{[ap + (1 - a)r]$ Pref q and q Pref $(bp + (1 - b)r)\}$ for some $0 < a,b < 1$ and for any measure r.

For a proof of the main "representation" theorem of Von Neumann–Morgenstern utility theory see Peter C. Fishburn, *Nonlinear Preference and Utility Theory* (Baltimore: Johns Hopkins University Press, 1988), sec. 1.3 and 1.4.

4. B. Skyrms, *The Dynamics of Rational Deliberation* (Cambridge, Mass.: Harvard University Press, 10.

5. Often these features of a medical procedure, or very similar features, such as the risk of death as a direct and early result of the procedure versus the length of life to be expected if the procedure "succeeds," are not separated when statistics are given for average survival after the procedure. They should be separated, as this example will make clear.

6. Think of "having" procedure A (for example) as having title to undergo it.

7. See R. Thaler, "Mental Accounting and Consumer Choice," *Marketing Science* 4 (1985): 199–214. The anecdotal evidence in this article is supplemented

by experimental evidence in R. Thaler and E. Johnson, "Gambling with the House Money and Trying to Break Even: The Effects of A Priori Outcomes on Risky Choice," *Management Science* 36 (1990): 643–660.

8. One theory to explain some of this keeping of separate accounts, for instance, the fact that people will earmark certain money for some special purpose and then literally never touch it for any other purpose, is that it is required for the psychological "technology of self-control." For a comparative assessment of a theory of this kind, and the standard economic theory of the consumer, in light of separate-accounts evidence, see Thaler, "Mental Accounting," and R. Thaler and H. Shefrin, "An Economic Theory of Self-Control," *Journal of Political Economy* 89 (1981): 392–406.

9. These functionals f must be skew-symmetric and bilinear. To say that f is skew-symmetric is to say that $f(p, q) = -f(q, p)$. To say that f is bilinear is to say that f is linear in each variable taken separately: For $0 < a < 1$,

$$f(ap + (1 - a)q, r) = af(p, r) + (1 - a) f(q, r), \text{ and:}$$
$$f(r, ap + (1 - a)q) = af(r, p) + (1 - a)f(r, q).$$

Thus, "SSB utility theory": "skew-symmetric, bilinear."

10. For a discussion of axioms for SSB utility theory, see Fishburn, *Nonlinear Preference and Utility Theory*, ch. 3 and 4.

11. See P. Fishburn, "Dominance in SSB Utility Theory," *Journal of Economic Theory* 34 (1984): 130–148, especially 136–138.

12. Susan has solved her theoretical problem in a way similar to the standard game theorist's move of considering "mixed strategies," with the added twist of a switch from standard expected utility theory to cycle-tolerant SSB utility theory.

13. Fishburn, *Nonlinear Preference and Utility Theory*, 44.

14. This objection is due to Teddy Seidenfeld. He also has concerns about the expense of creating the spinner acts—a factor that might devalue them as compared with the "ranking" assigned by SSB theory.

A PRIORI TRUTH

There is no algebraist nor mathematician so expert in his science, as to place entire confidence in any truth immediately upon his discovery of it, or regard it as anything but a mere probability. Every time he runs over his proofs his confidence increases; but still more by the approbation of his friends; and is raised to its utmost perfection by the universal assent and applauses of the learned world. Now it is evident that this gradual increase of assurance is nothing but the addition of new probabilities, and is derived from the constant union of causes and effects, according to past experience and observation.
—David Hume, *A Treatise of Human Nature*

Locke, Kant, the twentieth-century empiricists, and many other philosophers endorsed (or still endorse) the following four principles:

(1) Some propositions express facts such that if those facts did not obtain, nobody would be able to have precisely the concepts ingredient in the propositions. Examples: The algebraic group operation is associative. Red is not black.

(2) Reflection upon these concepts and reflection upon what is required in order to have just these concepts reveal that the propositions in question are true.

(3) Such propositions are knowable independently of experience because and only because of (2).

(4) Such propositions and only such propositions are a priori truths.

The conjunction of these four principles comprises what I shall call *classical apriorism*. Traditional proponents of classical apriorism would not all have used the technical jargon I have used in formulating (1)–(4). One must make adjustments—say, reading "idea" for "concept" and "truth of reason" for "a priori truth." The paradigm case of the a priori for this tradition is mathematical knowledge, and the epistemological role of classical apriorism dearest to its proponents has always been to explain why mathematical knowledge is incorrigible. The explanation is: Mathematical knowledge is incorrigible because mathematical truths are a priori.

Classical apriorism is incompatible with radical realism. Understand *radical realism* as the doctrine that there is a way things are in the world completely independent of how we represent the world in thought or language, together with the doctrine that the truth of a proposition is correspondence to this ultimate reality. Part of what is meant by 'completely independent of' here is that it is a possibility that we conceptually represent the world precisely as we do, and that every belief we have (perhaps excepting some privileged class—say, beliefs concerning our mental states) is false. Since classical apriorism places certain limits on how wrong we can be and still have the concepts with which we frame our right and wrong beliefs, a classical apriorist cannot consistently be a radical realist. I think there may be historical examples of this inconsistent stance—Locke, for one—but I shall not try to make out that case here.

I shall give an argument against classical apriorism, and supplement that argument with a redescription of the way in which mathematical truths can be known with a degree of certainty unmatched by truths of empirical science. This intuition is an ingredient in the intuition that mathematical knowledge is incorrigible; so accounting for it will help fill the gap left in our understanding of the special epistemological status of mathematics which is opened by a rejection of classical apriorism.

The argument I shall give against classical apriorism and the supplement to it I shall provide are fairly simple, and, in the case of the argument, shallow. The argument is shallow in that it consists in describing a counterexample with some straightforward stage setting and provides little by way of *diagnosis why* classical apriorism is false (although it provides some). W. V. Quine has developed a line of argument against classical apriorism which is deep in the way mine is shallow, and he has also supplemented this argument with an alternative account of one ingredient in the intuition that mathematical knowledge is incorrigible, although his ingredient is not the "certainty" ingredient with which I shall be concerned. I accept Quine's argument, and I think his supplement is plausible. My argument is intended to complement his, and my supplementary account of the intuition of certainty in mathematics is intended to complement his, in ways I shall now explain.

Quine has argued that classical apriorism is false because the activity described in (2) is not well defined and hence the claim made in (1) has no empirical significance. That is, he has argued that there is no distinction between having a concept of F which *requires*, say, that anything that is F is also G, and believing that all Fs are Gs. There is no fact of the matter whether coming to accept "Not all Fs are Gs" is changing one's meaning of 'F' in such a way that it no longer expresses the same concept, or just changing one's belief about Fs with no conceptual shift. So there is no such thing as "reflecting on what is required in order to have just these concepts," as (2) demands. The details of this argument are well known. It provides exactly the sort of diagnosis of what is wrong with classical apriorism that my argument does not provide.

On the other hand, there is not universal endorsement of Quine's argument, and part of the reason is this: People believe that, say, "All bachelors are unmarried" can be known incorrigibly, and this intuition is very strong. They do not see how any evidence could override their present grounds for accepting this proposition. This needs an explanation, and they seize upon the explanation that the proposition can be known incorrigibly because it is an a priori truth as characterized in classical apriorism. They are thus led to deny one or another Quinean premise needed in the argument against classical apriorism. If there is an independent argument against classical apriorism which does not depend on Quine's premises and which is not sensitive to the question whether "All bachelors are unmarried" can be known incorrigibly, this objection to his premises is unacceptable. *Then* Quine's argument, freed, as it were, from the rather simple job of refuting classical apriorism, can play the role of an explanation, and a deep explanation, of *why* that doctrine is wrong. The refutation by counterexample I shall describe is designed to do exactly this job.

As I said, Quine supplements his argument against classical apriorism with an explanation of the intuition that mathematical knowledge is incorrigible. His explanation is that mathematical truths are central in our conceptual scheme. Drastic revision of our mathematical beliefs would require so much revision in other beliefs that we literally cannot imagine what it would be like, psychologically, to hold such a massively revised belief set. He is right about that, and part of the common intuition that mathematical knowledge is incorrigible surely ought to be explained in just this way. But centrality does not explain one important part of the common intuition. We regard mathematical knowledge as especially certain, as knowledge arrived at in a way that leaves us especially unlikely to be mistaken. We think that, in any given case, the grounds a mathematician has for accepting a theorem he has proved constitute evidence for the theorem of an especially reliable kind. 'Kind' is the right word here, since we feel the difference between mathematical evidence and evidence in the empirical sciences as a difference in kind. Centrality does not explain this aspect of the intuition that mathematical knowledge is incorrigible. Even if the premises of a proof seem unrevisable to us because of their centrality, that does not explain why deriving a theorem from these premises should *in itself* seem to be an especially reliable way of establishing a belief.

I shall suggest an account of this intuition later. It will make use of some technical machinery I need anyway in order to describe the counterexample to classical apriorism. I shall develop the technical machinery in section I, describe the counterexample in section II, and finish in section III with my suggested reinterpretation of mathematical certainty.

I

We need a working explication of the notion of an a priori truth. I mean this to be an "explication" in Carnap's sense, a set of necessary and sufficient conditions for applying a term intuitively close in meaning to the term as commonly used, though precise where the usual meaning is vague. Explication thus involves legislation; in part I shall claim to have captured the traditional notion of an a priori truth, and in part I shall urge that our vague, intuitive notion be made precise in a certain way. The virtues of such an explication can be assessed by seeing to what degree it facilitates progress on previously unsolved or poorly understood philosophical problems.

Traditionally, 'a priori' has been used to label a kind of truth as well as to label a way of knowing. Because of the role of the a priori in empiricism and of Frege's influence in the philosophy of mathematics, the notion of an a priori *truth* has been the more important concept over the past century. Frege explicitly characterized apriority as a feature of truths, rather than as a feature of some person's knowledge of a truth. He put it this way (with a formalist bias thrown in):

> For a truth to be a posteriori, it must be impossible to construct a proof
> of it without including an appeal to facts, i.e., to truths which cannot
> be proved and are not general, since they contain assertions about

particular objects. But if, on the contrary, its proof can be derived exclusively from general laws, which themselves neither need nor admit of proof, then the truth is a priori.[1]

Recent empiricism had a misguided but well-articulated account of the nature of an a priori truth: Precisely the analytic truths are a priori. The concept of analyticity was examined with great care, but empiricists had relatively little to say about exactly how an analytic truth could be known or discovered "independently of experience." That a truth was analytic and that semantic conventions could be grasped "as internalized" presumably made plausible the claim that such a truth could be, and usually was known in a special, nonempirical way. So, both in Frege and in recent empiricism, the emphasis was on the a priori as a category of truth, not as a category of knowing, and I shall respect this emphasis by explicating the a priori as a kind of truth, a kind of knowable rather than a kind of knowledge.

The rest of the explication is no more than judicious conceptual engineering. I shall mark off the steps at places where differences of opinion about how to legislate are likely to arise.

a. We need a fundamental epistemic person-proposition relation. The best candidates are *having evidence for, being justified in accepting,* and *having enough experience to know.* The first is the natural choice for generating an explication of a priori truth and a neatly parallel explication of incorrigibility: Knowledge is incorrigible when the knower has evidence for the known proposition which could not be overridden by any additional evidence. One cannot describe the phenomenon of evidence overriding other evidence in any simple way in terms of either of the other two relations. It may be that one cannot do it all; that the evidence relation is conceptually very far removed from the other two, but I shall not argue that here. *Being justified in accepting* has the virtues and the vices of broadness. One can be justified in accepting what it pains one not to accept, or what one has promised a dying friend to accept, regardless of evidence. So reasonableness of believing, in a broad sense of 'reasonableness', and reasonableness of belief-content are not separated by describing someone as "justified in accepting a proposition." I think this is a good thing and permits us to be very flexible in whittling down justification in general to an appropriate sense of "epistemic" justification, although the whittling down must be done. I shall pick the third relation, *having enough experience to know*, sacrificing the advantages of the other two. I have reasons. First, it is an epistemic person-proposition relation which we can use in explicating a kind of "knowable" without encountering any version of Gettier's problem along the way. That is not true of the other choices. Second, I believe that the concept of having enough experience to know a proposition is older and fits more easily into the epistemologies of modern philosophers who were classical apriorists, whereas I believe that the evidence relation, and the "epistemic sense" of the justified acceptance relation are much newer inventions. I do not feel on very solid scholarly ground here, but it is what I believe. Here is an explication of that relation, as a preliminary move in explicating a priori truth:

> A person has enough experience to know a proposition if and only if that person's experience suffices for him to discover that the proposition is true given only further ratiocination.

b. Of course, when a person has acquired a certain amount of experience of all kinds, it is an idealization to suppose that he could *just think*, drawing in various ways on his past experiences but having from that time on only experiences of rational thought. In fact, a person who "goes on to think about" a proposition will do so amid a constant stream of further perceptual experiences, mood changes, ratiocination concerning other subjects, and so on. It may well be that what ratiocination a person is capable of during a given period of time will depend in part on what other experiences of all kinds he has. But we often do describe ourselves and others as having assimilated certain experiences, and then as having gone on to *just think* about a certain proposition on the basis of this past body of experience. And such a way of describing things is fundamental to all traditional conceptions of the a priori. So I'll recommend, provisionally, the following explication of "knowing independently of experience":

> *a* can know *p* *independently of experience* if and only if, in every metaphysically possible world in which *a* exists and *p* is true, *a* has enough experience to know *p*.

c. One obvious problem with this explication is that for any person there is a metaphysically possible world in which he dies before he has enough experience to know anything. So this first formulation is wrong. Intuitively, the relation a person bears to a proposition he can know independently of experience is this: No matter what course his life takes, if it is normal (he does not get dropped on his head) and long enough for his memory and other mental faculties to develop to the point where he *has the concepts in the proposition*, then he has enough experience to know it.

Having a concept and having the concepts "in a proposition" are notions tied so closely to the traditional conception of the a priori that we should use them in an explication of this sort. Replacing these notions by other devices, perhaps more philosophically intelligible devices, for capturing the idea that a person "grasps a proposition" might distort the resulting version of classical apriorism. At least I am unsure whether it would; so I suggest as a next step in explication:

> *a* can know *p* independently of experience if and only if in every world in which *a* exists, *p* is true, and *a* has the concepts in *p*, *a* has enough experience to know *p*.

This definition does not imply that *a* actually knows *p* in the worlds that meet the conditions set forth in the antecedent, but implies only that in such a world *a* has all the experience necessary *to come to know p* simply by ratiocination.

d. Classical apriorism usually restricts the a priori to those truths knowable independently of experience by everyone, thereby barring "I exist" and the like. I shall settle for the explication:

> (E) A truth *p* is a priori if and only if everyone can know *p* independently of experience.

It is possible to accommodate views according to which God and humans can know different classes of truths independently of experience, by complicating (E) with a relativization to "epistemological types" defined in an appropriate way. What is perhaps of more interest, it is possible to accommodate views according to which (i) different groups of people can know different classes of truths independently of experience, and (ii) it is literally impossible for people in one of these groups to acquire some of the concepts available to people in another of these groups (e.g., Americans/Tibetans, twentieth-century Europeans/fourteenth-century Europeans, schizophrenics of delusional-type T/nonschizophrenics, automata realizing Turing machine M/humans). Given a sorting into epistemological types, this will work for types other than the singleton type of which God is the only possible member:

(E′) A truth is a priori if and only if some member of some type can know p independently of experience, and, for all types and all metaphysically possible words, if a member of a type in a world can know p independently of experience, then any possible member of that type can likewise know p independently of experience in any world in which it exists.

How (E) should be modified to accommodate simultaneously what is a priori relative to Man, what is a priori relative to God, *and* the necessary uniqueness of God is left as an exercise for the devout reader. I shall use (E) hereafter as my explication of the a priori. Nothing I shall say is affected by omitting the complexities of (E′).[2]

II

Let me set the stage for a refutation of classical apriorism by noting a feature which is built into explication (E) quite intentionally but which I have not yet emphasized. I have explicated the concept of an a priori truth in a methodologically neutral way. By contrast, the category of a priori truth might be characterized as truth that can be discovered in a certain way—say, by "observing the agreement and disagreement of ideas," or by "introspecting internalized semantic conventions and testing for analyticity." On either of the two methodological characterizations I have just mentioned it would be plausible, at least prima facie, to reason that such a way of discovering truth is not a way of finding out about any particular possible world as opposed to any other. The outcome of such a procedure for finding truth should be insensitive to how things in fact are. One would thus expect a priori truths to be necessary.[3]

But I take it that classical apriorists who have described "a priori methods of discovery" (whatever jargon they may have used) have meant it to be a *substantive philosophical claim* that all truths discovered in such-and-such a way are a priori, with the category of a priori truth understood as "defined by" essentially the features I have built into my explication. Since this is so, there is no prima facie plausibility in the thesis that a priori truths are all necessary when the category of a priori truth is taken not as "defined by" some particular methodology, but rather as "defined by" (E). It is crucial to my argument that this interpretation of classical apriorism be acceptable. The counterexample I shall describe is a contingent proposition. Anyone who believes that necessity should be built into an explication of the concept of a priori truth will reject my refutation.

It is obvious that some contingent propositions qualify as a priori truths by the standards of (E)—"Something is conscious," for example, or "There are beings that engage in conceptual representation." These prepositions have a "Kantian necessity"—they are such that their truth is a necessary condition for knowledge (because it is a necessary condition for the existence of knowers). More to our point here, these propositions have the property described in clause (1) of classical apriorism. Their truth is a necessary condition for anyone's having the concepts in them. If we blind ourselves to Quine's arguments and think traditionally, it is just as obvious that (1) holds for the usual paradigms of necessary a priori truths. If "red is not black" were false, how could our concept of red be what it is? How could anyone have *this very concept* of red that we have? (Remember that a *radical* realist will deny this thesis, if he is consistent.)

Is clause (1) of classical apriorism true of all propositions that qualify as a priori truths when a priori truth is explicated by (E)? I shall argue that it is not, and thereby show that principles (1)–(4), which constitute classical apriorism, fail to characterize truths that are a priori according to (E). The reason for this failure can be clarified a little, though not in any deep way, if we approach the counterexample by way of a plausibility argument for clause (1), and locate the counterexample at the point where the argument fails. Here is the argument.

Consider an a priori truth p and a person a who can know p independently of experience. The metaphysically possible worlds in which a has the concepts in p and p is true are very diverse. And yet in every one of these diverse sets of circumstances, a can come to know p purely on the basis of ratiocination. This must be because a's having the concepts in p makes such ratiocination possible. Could a have the concepts in p in a world where p is false? If having the concepts in p makes such ratiocination possible, then if a could have the concepts in p in a world where p is false, such ratiocination would be possible in a world where p is false. Since a could give this very argument in a world where p is true, a could see that going through such a ratiocination process is compatible with the falsity of p. But anyone who backs off from accepting any of his ratiocinative conclusions for this reason is accepting radical realist skepticism full-blown. One might, then, take the preceding argument as a *reductio ad absurdum* of the assumption that if p is an a priori truth, it is possible for a to have the concepts in p in a world where p is false. Thus the conclusion of this *reductio* is clause (1) of classical apriorism. As I said, there is a flaw in this argument for either radical realist skepticism or classical apriorism. The flaw is the assumption that the truth of *p* cannot affect *a*'s ability to know *p* except by affecting *a*'s ability to have the concepts in *p*. It ignores the fact that the truth of an a priori truth might affect the ability of knowers to exercise enough "pure reason" to know the proposition even if they have the relevant concepts.

I shall adopt the Postal Service Convention of reporting the four-color theorem as "four colors suffice." Now consider the proposition:

P: It is physically possible to prove that four colors suffice.

Assume that P is true in *W*, and *a* has the concepts in P in *W*. Then, in *W*, *a* can know that four colors suffice independently of experience because he can prove it. Then, appealing to an obvious modal principle, he can infer from the fact that he has a proof that in his world it is physically possible to prove it. The same will hold for any knower who has the concepts in P in a world in which P is true; so P is an a priori truth.

Now consider a world *W*★ where P is false. Say some knower *b* has the concepts in P in *W*★. But, because of the physical laws of *W*★, every creature disintegrates in a shorter period of time than it takes to prove that four colors suffice. We know that one proof that four colors suffice takes a very long time to run through, and if every proof of the theorem is similarly complicated, it is easy to imagine that the time required for any human to complete the proof much exceeds the time required for a human to acquire the concepts "four," "color," and "suffices." Nothing turns on this particular choice of example; it merely makes the logical situation easier to imagine common-sensically. The upshot is that, although *b* has the concepts in P in *W*★, P is false in *W*★. Although P is an a priori truth, it is false that, in any possible situation in which someone has the concepts in P, P is true. The reason, of course, is that the truth of P is a necessary condition for anyone to engage in *enough ratiocination* to know P. So the truth of an a priori proposition is not, in general, a necessary condition for anyone's having the concepts in it.

There is an objection to my argument along the following lines: The inference one makes from the fact that one has a proof of a theorem to the conclusion that it is physically possible to prove it, although made according to an a priori modal principle, has a non-a-priori premise. The premise is that one has a proof of the theorem. On what grounds could we argue that this premise is not a priori? Possibly on the grounds that to know that one has a proof of a proposition one has to remember that one has proved it, and that a report *that you remember* proving a theorem is never a priori true. But this move just converts my argument against classical apriorism into a dilemma. Mathematics is a paradigm for classical apriorism. If the objection to my argument is sustained, almost no mathematical proposition is an a priori truth. Nearly all mathematical knowledge requires accepting, as reasons for accepting some theory, propositions analogous to "I proved lemma L earlier" or "I remember that lemma L has been established."

Some philosophers of mathematics—Frege, for instance—have written as though the epistemology of mathematics, unlike the epistemology of everything else, should make reference only to *mathematical* propositions and not to such propositions as "I constructed a good proof of L_9 from two lemmas I proved last week." A mathematician's evidence for accepting a theorem is idealized as isomorphic to a formal proof—a sequence of "steps," each a *mathematical* proposition. This was Frege's reason for rejecting Schroeder's suggestion for an "Axiom of Symbolic Stability," which "guarantees us that throughout all our arguments and deductions the symbols remain constant in our memory—or preferably on paper." Frege (*op. cit.*, introduction) thought Schroeder confused the "grounds" of proof with the mental or physical conditions to be satisfied if the proof is to be given. Imagine an epistemologist of perception saying that my evidence for "This is a tomato" may include "This is red" but *not* "I have not forgotten how red things look under these conditions." In fact the body of accepted propositions a mathematician must know to be true (and which must not be overridden) in order to be justified in accepting a theorem nearly always includes *much* more than "purely mathematical" propositions.

Someone who believed that mathematical knowledge (unlike empirical knowledge or knowledge of one's mental states) is grounded solely on the apprehension of concepts would tend to think that all that is necessary for mathematical knowledge is possession of the relevant concepts, together with enough general understanding to think one's way to the proposition in question. Thus the need for people to engage in the psychological process of ratiocination in order to prove theorems is ignored, as is the possibility of propositions that are about a ratiocinative process, or propositions whose truth or falsity would imply something about the actual following of the pathway. Rather, ratiocination is treated as if it were simply entailment in logical space. Consider Frege's definition of an a priori truth (quoted in section 1 earlier). When Frege says that an a priori truth is a truth that can be derived exclusively from general laws, he means that in an abstract structure of proofs, such a derivation exists. But it doesn't follow that a human being, or any other conscious being, could ever deduce that proposition from general laws. Usually such considerations are avoided by invoking the idealization of an infinite knower. Once this move is made, however, it is unclear how the notion of an a priori truth could play a role in explaining the incorrigibility of mathematical knowledge. It is mainly by confusing derivations and derivings, the former a propositional content, the latter a real event, that philosophers can maintain their classical apriorism on the one hand and on the other hand believe it can be used to explain the incorrigibility of mathematics.

III

Among classical apriorists, it has been traditional to assume that being a priori entails being incorrigibly knowable, where we may take as a working explication of "incorrigibility" the familiar "S knows p incorrigibly if and only if the evidence S has for p could not be overridden by any additional evidence." What I have said about mathematics and memory suggests that there is a problem with the view that mathematics is incorrigible in this sense. Since a mathematician's total evidence for some theorem typically includes many such propositions as "I remember that lemma L has been established," such total evidence could be overridden by various unexpected information about oneself; e.g., that one usually misremembers topological statements of more than six words. Nevertheless, there remains the intuition mentioned in section 1 above—the intuition that the evidence mathematicians have for their mathematical knowledge renders that knowledge so much more certain than empirical knowledge that the difference is a "difference in kind." Traditionally the difference has been "philosophically explained" (i.e., philosophically elucidated) by the supposed incorrigibility of mathematical knowledge, and the supposed incorrigibility of mathematical knowledge has in turn been philosophically explained by the conjunctive claim that mathematical truths are a priori, classical apriorism is true, and classical apriorism shows why anything a priori is incorrigibly knowable. Since either classical apriorism is false or most mathematics is not a priori, this will not do.

I suggest a compromise. We should reject the incorrigibility of mathematical knowledge. We should philosophically explain the certainty of mathematical knowledge as due to a very great difference between the properties of mathematical errors, and, e.g., those of errors in the empirical sciences. Finally, we should construe "ratiocination" in my explanation of the a priori broadly enough to count mathematical truths as a priori in the event they are provable, and treat mathematical truth as the *defining stereotype* for a priori truth. Let me explain:

Consider a mathematician who is proceeding through a proof. He has proved lines L_7 and L_8, and he says (or thinks) line L_9, which follows validly from L_7 and L_8. But he does not remember whether he proved L_7 or simply assumed it as a hypothesis. Observers he has every reason to trust tell him he did not prove L_7. Clearly he has insufficient evidence to justify his accepting L_9, though he has proved it. Of course, this example presumes an especially feeble memory, but no human can hold all of a very complicated mathematical theory in mind. One must trust memories, one must trust that symbols in a notebook have not been changed so as to mislead, and one must trust textbooks and colleagues at least as supports for one's own apparent memories. In general, the evidence possessed by a mathematician for a theorem can be overridden by any of a great variety of further evidential inputs.

If we accept Cartesian incorrigibility of the mental, we can consider just some part of mathematics which a given human can do by holding every premise and every inferential move in a proof "present to the mind," and arguably, that part of mathematics will be incorrigibly known by that human when he has finally reached the point of grasping it all at once. Of course, this will be a tiny part of mathematics. In general, mathematical knowledge is not incorrigible. Is it not odd, then, that mathematics has been accorded privileged status as an a priori science?

It is not odd. The "empirical" mistakes a mathematician can make are (or were before machine theorem-proving entered the picture) different from the mistakes open to other scientists in two important ways. They are *technologically simple* to look for, and they are plausibly supposed to be *unsystematic*. A clerical error, misprint, or faulty memory can be discovered by easy checking procedures available at all times to a mathematician and to his research community. Bubble chambers are hard to fix and hard to be sure are still fixed; even small mistakes in weighing chemicals are much harder to catch than a mistaken writing of 'α' for 'a'.

And mistakes due to faulty inferential thinking or faulty memory do not, so we believe, occur systematically throughout the mathematical community. Where I slip up, you will not. The idiosyncratic weakness of my habits of mind will not be generally shared. If mathematics were done in isolation or if there were *many* cases of trick proofs that tend to seduce everyone alike, *our attitudes would be very different*. Natural scientists are not so well off. Everybody who watches the amoebas divide in microscope illumination may see them divide in two, when in fact they divide in three in the dark. Delicate indirect testing is needed to show that *all* biologists are not systematically misled in such ways. It might be right to say that the very heart of natural science is uncovering the respects in which nature systematically fools every observer alike until observations of an especially clever design finally show us the truth.

These differences between mathematics and natural science are the foundation of our intuition that mathematical knowledge is especially *certain*, and completely justify preferential treatment for mathematics. It *should* be called an a priori science. And it should be the *stereotypical* system of a priori knowledge. The way to get that effect, given my explication of the a priori, is to treat looking something up in a different book, or noticing that you tend to make algebraic mistakes when you are hungry though not otherwise, as part of "ratiocination." Neither phenomenon would ordinarily be counted as an exercise of pure reason. That is sensible enough. These are not exercises of pure reason taken by themselves, or as part of larger sequences of experience which have a claim to the title "ratiocination." My suggestion is that such experiences should be counted as elements in ratiocinative thought when (a) we must so count them in order to make everything evidentially relevant to a given piece of mathematical knowledge turn out to be pure ratiocination, or (b) when they occur in some sequence of experiences which though it does not lead to mathematical knowledge, is intuitively *very like* some experience-sequence that would lead to mathematical knowledge, and which does lead to the having of some piece of knowledge about something, and in which the experience in question must be included so as to include everything evidentially relevant to the piece of knowledge in question. That is, what is a priori should be adjusted to fit what is done in actual mathematical practice. In the correct epistemological order, it should not be a *discovery* that the truths of mathematics are a priori. What should be a discovery is that some truths of some other subject matters are a priori, i.e., "mathlike."

My articulation of what is to count as ratiocination is vague insofar as it is always *somewhat* a matter of opinion when something is "very like" something else, but I believe the concept of an a priori truth, like the concept of "worth buying," is more useful if it is left vague in that way.

My argument that mathematics should work as a defining stereotype of the a priori is very simple. Besides the community of mathematicians, there is no other easily individuated community of intellectual inquirers whose empirical errors qua members of that community have the important properties I noted—the technological ease with which these errors can be discovered, and the unsystematic occurrence of these errors. Both properties, and especially the second, are properties an error has relative to the practices *of a community*. Being prey only to empirical errors with these properties is a remarkable epistemological credential. It is, or makes for, "certainty," and there should be a philosophical device to pick it out when it occurs away from the mathematical practices of mathematicians. I think that is what the category of a priori truth should do. With classical apriorism false, it has nothing else to do.

Notes

George Boolos, Sylvain Bromberger, Richard Cartwright, Carl Ginet, Alan Hazen, Thomas Nagel, Carl Posy, Richmond Thomason, Judith Thomson, and Joseph Camp all helped me greatly with their criticisms of earlier drafts of this essay and with suggestions for improvement. My research was supported by a summer stipend from the National Endowment for the Humanities and a Mellon Postdoctoral Fellowship at the University of Pittsburgh.

1. Gottlob Frege, *The Foundations of Arithmetic*, tr. J. L. Austin (New York: Oxford University Press, 1950), 4.

2. According to (E'), which truths are a priori will depend on one's metaphysics. If there are knowers with infinite minds, some truths would be a priori, which would not be if one countenanced only knowers with finite minds. This is as it should be, since what truths are knowable at all is partly a metaphysical question. Epistemology can decide what the conditions are in which someone *would* know something. But whether these conditions *could* obtain may be a question for science, or in other cases, for metaphysics.

3. This is essentially Saul Kripke's formulation in "Naming and Necessity," in *Semantics of Natural Language*, ed. D. Davidson and G. Harman (Dordrecht: Reidel, 1972), 263; also published independently (Cambridge, Mass.: Harvard University Press, 1980), 38.

4

STIPULATION AND
EPISTEMOLOGICAL PRIVILEGE

I

Empiricists, especially twentieth-century empiricists, have typically accepted a certain conventionalist epistemological doctrine. The doctrine can be put as follows. The meaning of a predicate can be stipulated by definition. When this is done, the people who have given the definitions, as well as anyone who understands the definitions, come to have two epistemological privileges. They can know the truth of certain statements about the world "independently of experience," or "a priori," or "without empirical investigation." And they can know these statements to be true incorrigibly; that is, with a degree of assurance that no evidence gained by empirical observation could override. Both of these privileges supposedly result from the fact that if, say, I have stipulated that sets are to be called 'totally ordered' if and only if they have the properties G and H, I can then know that all totally ordered sets are G simply by reflecting upon my stipulative convention. This requires no empirical investigation, so I have the first privilege. All it does require is scrutiny of my own mental states, in this case my having mentally accepted a rule for applying a term, and all such judgments about one's own immediate mental states can be known incorrigibly according to the Cartesian tradition upon which empiricism was built. I shall call precisely the view I have just described "empiricist conventionalism."

It was also typical of empiricism to treat *all* meaningful predicates as though they had been stipulatively defined, so that the simple this-is-what-it-means definitions of terms in a mathematics textbook were viewed as paradigm cases of linguistic conventions in general. This over-simplified conception of the system of conventions which give a term meaning in a natural language led empiricists to extend the epistemo-logical privileges supposedly available in the case of stipulatively defined terms to the general case of all meaningful predicates, including such favorites as 'bachelor', which almost certainly was never stipulatively defined. "Analytic" truths were everywhere, and knowledge both a priori and incorrigible could be had on literally any subject. It might be boring, but it was easy to get and unshakeably grounded.

Attacks on the notion of analyticity by Quine, Putnam, and others have been almost entirely attacks on the empiricist assimilation of all predicate meaning to the case of stipulated predicate meaning. For instance, if many predicates in fact express law-cluster concepts, they will not have inter-nalizable definitions that enable someone to enjoy the epistemological privileges just mentioned. Recent attacks on the empiricists' philosophy of language have *not* been attacks on the more limited doctrine I am calling empiricist conventionalism, the doctrine that *stipulative definition* can, in principle, enable language-users to have a priori and incorrigible knowledge of the extramental world at a very cheap price.[1] It is thus no surprise to find a close analogue of empiricist conventionalism emerging in recent work on the philosophy of language by Kripke, Donnellan, and others. The new doctrine concerns the stipulation of referents for names and other singular terms, rather than meanings of predicates. But it is the same old doc-trine nonetheless, or so I shall argue. I shall also argue that the new con-ventionalist doctrine is false. I believe very similar arguments would show the empiricist conventionalist doctrine false in the case of stipulated predi-cate meaning as well, but I shall not give those arguments here.

II

Saul Kripke will be my star example of a new conventionalist. But before discussing Kripke's views I want to lay some of the groundwork for my reply by switching to an idea due to Gerald Massey.[2] Massey charac-terizes some predicates as "preceptive."

Preceptive predicates are a class of predicates whose reference is de-termined in a way rather like what goes on with proper names or demon-stratives but that, arguably, have an ordinary "intensional" component of meaning invariant through changes in reference-fixing policy. There are many examples of such predicates, for example, "illegal," "x-rated," "married," "out" or "safe." What is illegal and what is not will vary from occasion to occasion, according to the lawmaking activity of legislators, and who is out or safe will vary from occasion to occasion, according to the calls of umpires. But 'illegal', unlike 'John' or 'this', has a fixed meaning. Such predicates are particularly important in revealing the relation between linguistic conventions and conventions of other sorts.

Massey describes a case in which an appropriate officer declares some place off limits. If Katie's Bar is thus declared off limits, it is. The soldiers involved cannot know independently of empirical observation, or know incorrigibly, that Katie's Bar is off limits. They have to read the proper announcement, or make certain other inquiries. Can the colonel, when he declares Katie's Bar off limits, know independently of experience, or know incorrigibly, that it is?

The answer is that he cannot, despite the fact that he knows that Katie's Bar is off limits partly in virtue of conventional legislation on his part. His knowledge is interestingly different from his knowledge that rocks are hard because of this conventional element. He must know certain rules and know how to apply them. But that does not make his knowledge independent of empirical investigation or incorrigible, because he must also know that the rules have been properly applied, and that requires a great deal of empirical observation.

Consider an enlisted man who wonders whether he will be arrested if he goes to Katie's Bar. He might reason as follows.

(1) The MPs will raid Katie's Bar this evening.

(2) Colonel Jones has declared in way X that Katie's Bar is off limits.

(3) Colonel Jones is entitled to classify an establishment off limits by declaring in way X that it is off limits.

(4) So Katie's Bar is off limits.

(5) If an establishment is off limits, is raided by the MPs, I am in the establishment, and the MPs are dutiful, then the MPs will throw me in the stockade.

(6) The MPs are dutiful.

(7) So if the MPs raid Katie's Bar this evening and I am there, I will be thrown in the stockade.

In this reasoning, (3) is known by knowing rules and knowing that a certain person is licensed, under the rules, to legislate in a certain way.

One could be mistaken about either thing, but it is arguable that this is not an empirical mistake in the case of knowing the rules, and not a *purely* empirical mistake in the case of knowing that Colonel Jones is licensed to declare places off limits, though some empirical investigation would be required to know the latter. (6) is likewise a statement about how the rules are being applied. Knowing (6) requires knowing the rules and observing that certain people who play certain rule-established roles are in fact doing what the rules prescribe. (5) is a kind of translevel conditional, its antecedent employing several rule-governed concepts (off limits, dutiful), and its consequent purely nonnormative. Perhaps to know (5) it is enough to know the rules and to know how to think. (1) is discharged by conditionalization, but (2) remains a matter for perfectly ordinary empirical observation. So if a soldier reasons his way to (7) in this way, he must make observations of the world at several points along the way, and he can be wrong. That is why we do not think he knows (7) incorrigibly or in any sense independently of experience, although his knowledge is based in considerable part on his awareness of conventions.

The important point is that although Colonel Jones gave the order, Colonel Jones does not know nonempirically or incorrigibly that Katie's Bar is off limits either. From an epistemological point of view, he is in the same position as an enlisted man. If Colonel Jones wants to infer (7), he must make exactly the same observations of the world. He must determine that the rules make him a person licensed to declare places off limits, and that will involve some empirical observation (e.g., checking to see if certain orders are indeed addressed to him). And he must determine, empirically, that (2) is true. Doing that may be easier for him than for the enlisted man, but it is still empirical observation. He is in the same situation as a participant in a marriage ceremony. The groom, say, can make it be the case that he is married by saying "I do," but he must make empirical observations in order to know that he is married, or in order to know some nonnormative facts that depend upon his being married. He must know that events have occurred throughout the ceremony of the type specified by the rules, so that he knows when he is licensed to make himself be married by saying "I do." And he must know that he has said it.

That is why we do not think such a person can know when he is married incorrigibly or without empirical observation. And it is why we do not think that a baseball umpire can know when a ball is fair, or know the nonnormative consequences of that, incorrigibly or without empirical observation, even though the umpire can make it be that a ball is fair by gesturing in the appropriate way. We do not think the umpire or the groom are any more able to know these things nonempirically or incorrigibly than the spectators are. That is because the umpire, for instance, is only slightly better positioned to know what gesture he has made than a spectator is, and he is only slightly better positioned to know that (and when) he is licensed by the rules to make something be the case by performing an act. The umpire might know nonempirically that he intended to call the ball fair, and there are those who believe that he knows incorrigibly that he intended to do this. But nobody would confuse this with the claim that he knows nonempirically or incorrigibly that he has succeeded.

In the case of performances that assign meanings or referents to words, however, philosophers frequently fail to notice the relevance of exactly these considerations.

III

Consider the following suggestion of Saul Kripke.

> Neptune was hypothesized as the planet which caused such and such discrepancies in the orbits of certain other planets. If Leverrier indeed gave the name 'Neptune' to the planet before it was ever seen, then he fixed the reference of 'Neptune' by means of the description just mentioned. At that time he was unable to see the planet even through a telescope. At this stage an *a priori* material equivalence held between the statements 'Neptune exists' and 'some one planet perturbing the orbit of such and such other planets exists in such and such a position', and also such statements as 'if such and such perturbations are caused by a planet, they are caused by Neptune' had the status of *a priori* truths.[3]

Kripke's astronomer supposedly knows this biconditional:

> (1) Neptune exists if and only if some one planet perturbing the orbit of such and such other planets exists in such-and-such a position.

Kripke's discussion, here and elsewhere, makes it clear that he thinks this because he thinks knowing (I) in virtue of having engaged in the reference-fixing puts the astronomer in a privileged epistemic position. So far as I can tell, the astronomer is supposed to have precisely these two privileges, both of them obvious analogues of the privileges accorded to predicate-definers by empiricist conventionalism:

> (i) The astronomer knows (I) solely in virtue of having internalized the convention he himself established, so he does not know (I) on the basis of any empirical observation.
>
> (ii) Because of (i), the astronomer's grounds for accepting (I) could not be overridden by any additional empirical evidence.[4]

Neither (i) nor (ii) is true.

It takes some empirical observation to discover, in many cases, that you are licensed to name something in the public language. In fact (so I am told) an astronomer is licensed to name a planet he discovers, but to know he is so licensed he not only has to know the rule, he has to know he discovered the planet. Once again, if we restrict our attention to the idiolect, the rule may be that you can do what you want. But even if you do not have to make empirical observations to discover that you are licensed to assign meanings or referents to words in your idiolect, you still have to make empirical observations to discover that you have done it. To see this, consider the following analogue of the off limits reasoning, leading to the conclusion that if there is a unique planet causing the perturbations, Neptune is that planet. I will give the reasoning in a form that is appropriate to someone who has baptized Neptune "for us"—that is, for our sublanguage of the public language, because I suspect that is really what Kripke had in mind.

> (1) There is a unique planet that causes the perturbations.
>
> (2) I have announced in way X that the unique planet causing the perturbations is to be called 'Neptune' by us.
>
> (3) I am entitled to name a planet 'Neptune' for us by announcing in way X that it is to be so named.
>
> (4) So the unique planet that causes the perturbations is named 'Neptune' for us.
>
> (5) If a planet p is named 'Neptune' for us, and we are participating in our talk, then it is true for us to say 'Neptune causes the perturbations' if and only if p causes the perturbations.
>
> (6) We are participating in our talk.
>
> (7) So it is true for us to say 'Neptune causes the perturbations.'
>
> (8) If it is true for us to say 'Neptune causes the perturbations' then Neptune causes the perturbations.

(9) So if there is a unique planet that causes the perturbations, then Neptune causes the perturbations.

The only difference between this argument and the off limits argument is the added steps (7) and (8) before the conclusion. Anyone who thinks (8) is trivial will think the arguments exactly analogous. Once again, the premises are an epistemological mixture. (5) may be knowable just by understanding the rules governing our linguistic practice. But (3) is a matter of knowing that I am licensed by those rules to name planets by performing certain acts. That requires some empirical observation—in this case, probably, finding out whether others of us are willing to go along. And (2) is a plain empirical matter of fact. Knowing it has nothing to do with knowing rules, any more than the umpire can tell when his arm has shot out by knowing the rules of baseball.

So there are places where I do depend on observation to know (9), and consequently there are places in my reasoning where my beliefs can be overridden by new empirical observations. So (i) and (ii) are false on the face of them. Why does Kripke think otherwise? My diagnosis is that he does two things. First he thinks of reference-fixing for the public language, or for "our-talk," as though it were like reference-fixing for one's idiolect. This makes him overlook the need to determine (partly by empirical observation) that (3) is true, that I am a "licensed namer." And it makes him ignore the possibility that (6) requires some empirical investigation—say, to determine whether we are all intending our noisemaking to be speech. Second, still confusing public language with idiolect, he thinks the naming performance can be done mentally, silently, inwardly. And he thinks one's own conscious states and acts are incorrigibly knowable and also knowable without "outward" empirical investigation. So although observation is indeed required to know (2), it is a special, privileged observation that does not depend upon extramental empirical discoveries, and the results of which could not be overturned by further empirical discoveries. *That* is the sense in which the astronomer is privileged, and that is the ground for Kripke's acceptance of (i) and (ii).

IV

It would be possible to attack this position by arguing that it is false that one can know one's mental states independently of any extramental investigation, and also false that one can know one's mental states incorrigibly. But I want to emphasize that the position is false *whether or not* Cartesian views on privileged access to the mental are correct. So I shall assume for purposes of argument that our hypothetical Neptune-namer does his naming completely mentally, and that he does know a priori and incorrigibly that he has performed this mental act. *It does not follow* that he knows a priori and incorrigibly that the biconditional (I) is true. That is what really matters, since the biconditional reports an extramental fact, and the striking claim made by all forms of conventionalism is that by internalizing linguistic rules one can know, and know in specially privileged ways, *extramental* and *nonnormative* facts, such as that bachelors are all unmarried, or in the case at hand the fact expressed by biconditional (I).

To see why the astronomer has no epistemological privilege with respect to (I), suppose after he has done his purely mental act of naming he tells others about his invention of the name and it passes into common use in the public language. Soon a planet is seen through a telescope at roughly the position predicted. People say "Neptune has been sighted." Later the planet is reached by spacecraft, and people say "Neptune has been explored and colonized." About thirty years after the name was introduced, revolutionary developments in planetary mechanics make it clear that in fact Neptune never had anything to do with the famous orbital perturbations. Everyone decides that the biconditional (I) is false and *always was*. They would be right; it would be the only intuitively plausible assessment of (I). However famous the original baptizer was, when he believed biconditional (I), he was wrong.

Clearly all this could happen. So in order to know at the time of the original naming that (I) was true, the astronomer would have to have good reason to believe things will not develop as I have described. He certainly has such reason, if only because he has good reason to believe planetary mechanics is not all *that* wrong. But he has knowledge of such things as planetary mechanics on the basis of lots of extramental empirical observations, and certainly does not have it incorrigibly. So even if we concede that he can know incorrigibly and without the help of any extramental empirical observation that he has performed a mental act of naming, he *cannot know biconditional (I)* in a similar privileged way.

It is tempting to fight for the conventionalist position by claiming that somewhere along the line the term 'Neptune' changed its reference;

specifically that it was an empty name when first mentally invented, since the description in the right-hand side of (I) did not really apply to anything. Later that empty name came to refer to a planet.

But since the scenario I described is intuitively plausible, a claim of reference-shift needs special defense. One might try arguing that in my scenario the original inventor of the name cannot be regarded as having *then* used it to refer to the planet Neptune because when he performed his silent baptism he had no way to "pick out," or "apprehend," or "individuate" a referent for the term except as whatever, if anything, fit the description in (I). Since nothing did fit that description, the name for him at that moment was empty.

This reply is wrong. As Donnellan and Kripke have argued convincingly, people do not need a way of picking out or descriptively individuating some object in order to use a name to refer to that object. Someone can use 'Margaret Thatcher' to refer, as we all do, to a particular woman even if the person has never seen, heard, or touched Margaret Thatcher and can only describe her, wrongly, as "the president of England." The inventor of the name 'Neptune' was, in my hypothetical scenario, just one more member of a community of users of that name spread out both temporally and spatially. The standards of that community control name reference in the public language, and in my scenario the community uses the name to refer to a planet. The original inventor of the name introduced it into common usage, and he is as bound by that usage as anyone else. If his position as temporally first user of the name exempts him from being so bound, *much* more argument is needed to show why.

It would be a clumsy thesis in any event. When, precisely, did 'Neptune' stop being an empty name? When somebody applied it to a planet seen through a telescope? And if the original name-inventor didn't look through the telescope or hear about the observation for a few days, was *he* using 'Neptune' as an empty name, unlike some of his colleagues until . . . until what? Until they told him? Until he looked through the telescope?

Of course there is a simple way to disconnect the name-inventor from public language conventions, at least for a while. Just suppose that when he engaged in his inward, mental act of naming he also *decided*, all in his mind, always to use the name 'Neptune' to refer to whatever, if anything, caused certain orbital perturbations. Granting, as I still am, a Cartesian view of priviliged access to the mental, we could claim that he knows independently of extramental experience and also knows incorrigibly that he has performed the naming *and* that he has decided to have *his* use of the name forever controlled by a sort of defining constraint. If everybody else lets that constraint submerge slowly under other constraints on the name's usage, he will not do so.

The problem, of course, is that although he may know a priori and incorrigibly that he has made this mental decision, he cannot know either a priori or incorrigibly that he will stick to it. He might even forget the decision a few seconds later, which is not importantly different from his never having made the decision at all. If the scenario I described followed an initial invention of the name 'Neptune' that happened to involve a few seconds of commitment to an ineffectual policy to reserve the name only for a certain sort of planet, absolutely nothing would be changed. People would celebrate the discovery that Neptune doesn't really affect the orbit of anything, remark that until recently everybody thought it did, and find nothing paradoxical in the fact that the great Leverrier himself, the man who gave Neptune its name, was as wrong as everybody else.

V

At this point a conventionalist might reply that my argument depends upon understanding "idiolect" a certain way. I have been construing a speaker's idiolect as just the specific *version* of the public language used by that speaker. So the reference of some name "in an idiolect" is still controlled by public standards of usage, which—admittedly—are not under the control of any single member of a language community. But surely this is not charitable to the conventionalist position. The charitable understanding of "idiolect" would disconnect the referential conventions of a speaker's "idiolect" from the referential conventions of the public language. Or better, since nothing quite that drastic is required, we should allow that any particular name may be *given a private reference* by a speaker, while the rest of the speaker's expressions remain subject to public semantic standards. To give a private reference to a name is simply to establish a rule for its correct referential usage, which rule binds the speaker to so use the name, does not bind anyone else to so use it, and can be established or dissolved only by the speaker.

Then I can give the name 'Bob' a private reference. I can decide that its private reference will be the sheet of yellow paper on which I am writing. And I can do this silently and inwardly, so that my knowledge that I have done it is incorrigible by traditional Cartesian lights. *Now*, finally, I shall have produced a stipulative definition that enables me to have incorrigible knowledge of a nonlinguistic fact, the fact that if there exists a unique yellow sheet of paper on which I am writing (or, timelessly, . . . "am writing at time t . . .'), then Bob exists. Even if others find out about the private reference I have given 'Bob', and even after some time it is generally accepted that something else is and always was correctly called 'Bob', that will not matter. That will be a fact about the public reference of 'Bob'. The private reference I have given to 'Bob' will be unaffected. So the argument I gave earlier in the case of 'Neptune' cannot be repeated, and could not have been given in the case of Leverrier and 'Neptune' if I had been charitable enough to construe Leverrier's stipulate definition as having given 'Neptune' a private reference.

This conventionalist reply faces an objection in the spirit of Wittgenstein's attack on "private languages." The conventionalist's suggestion is that by declaring that I will call thing X 'Bob', or undertaking to thereafter call thing X 'Bob', I establish a rule of correct referential usage for 'Bob' that governs my future use of the name until I dissolve the rule for myself. I suggest that this is a contingent hypothesis about myself, which I cannot know incorrigibly, whether the declaring or undertaking is done inwardly or outwardly.

Obviously some people name things in private. They name pets, cars, household appliances, and even people. Often this sort of pet-naming is done in company with others, but it can be done alone. If it is done alone and the pet-namer has a good memory for such things, the name will have a rule-governed usage in the pet-namer's language. If the pet-namer insists that the referent he originally established for the pet name is always its referent *for him*, this is a perfectly ordinary and philosophically defensible claim. It is a "claim" in the sense of a request to be accorded a right, as well as a "claim" in the sense of an assertion, because the pet-namer is asking that his usage of the name be regarded by other members of his public language community as correctly applying to the thing he named, regardless whether the name also happens to pass into public usage with different (or additional) rules for its correct use. In fact we respect such claims, so that much of the conventionalist's suggestion is defensible.

But it is just as obvious that not every ceremonial utterance of a term in a way that is somehow related to a thing establishes a private reference for the term. My saying "Bob" while in the same house as thing X does not make thing X the private referent of 'Bob' for me. My wondering whether 'Bob' would be a good name for thing X does not make thing X the private referent of 'Bob' for me. In both cases, the ceremony, whether performed aloud or inwardly and mentally, fails to establish a rule of referential usage because it fails to produce a necessary condition for such a rule to be in effect: namely, that I am thereafter disposed to use the term 'Bob' in response to thing X under a range of appropriate conditions. What count as appropriate conditions are determined by our concept of reference. That I respond to a typical visual perception of thing X with the term 'Bob' counts as appropriate. That I respond with the word 'Bob' when asked "What are some of the possible names for thing X you've been considering?" does not count as appropriate. Recent work on reference has made it clear that appropriate conditions are more varied than was once believed. For the term 'Gödel' in the public language English, for example, that I respond with 'Gödel' when asked for the name of the semiliterate janitor who rose to undeserved fame by printing and publishing brilliant mathematical essays, given that I have discovered certain surprising facts about the history of mathematics, counts as appropriate. For a ceremony to establish thing X as the referent of 'Bob' for me it is necessary, though not sufficient, that engaging in the ceremony causally result in my having a substantial number of appropriate response-dispositions.

The normal pet-namer's undertaking to use a certain name for a certain thing satisfies this necessary condition. But not every undertaking to use a certain name for a certain thing does. Consider a child who plays imaginative and rapidly changing games with toy people. Even within a game, the child sets the toy people in various arrangements to play according to various quickly shifting rules, since he does not have enough toy people to make up even one starship crew or football team. He says "You're Darth Vader" to one of them a few seconds before repositioning it and saying "You're Luke Skywalker" to it. Sometimes *even as he is saying* "You're Darth Vader" to a toy person he is changing his mind in the sense that he will not even for a few seconds treat it as representing Darth Vader, and will not settle on what to call it next until a few more seconds have elapsed. It is active, somewhat wild play. (One could tell a similar story about a manic adult engaging in a frenzy of *apparent* pet-naming and pet-renaming.)

In some cases the child's declarations, or undertakings to name, will result in very short-term appropriate dispositions to respond with a certain name to a certain toy person. But in other cases, as when the child is shifting into another assignment of roles even as he declares a certain toy person to have a certain name, no such response-disposition will result. So in these cases, the child will not have established even briefly a private reference for the name.

We cannot know incorrigibly, although we *can* know, whether we are like the normal reclusive pet-namer or like the child. We can only know this by empirical observation of ourselves and others relevantly like us. So we cannot know incorrigibly whether an undertaking to use a term to refer to a certain thing has causally produced appropriate response-dispositions. So we cannot know incorrigibly whether an undertaking to use a term to refer to a certain thing has established a private rule of correct referential usage. So I cannot know incorrigibly that if there exists a unique yellow piece of paper on which I am writing then Bob exists, even if I inwardly undertake to call 'Bob' exactly what fits that description. I know I can adopt such a private reference for the term 'Bob' because I know I am not like the child. But I only know that because I have empirical experience of myself that goes far beyond my immediate awareness of present subjective states. Thus the conventionalist's retreat into privacy of referential standards does not save him.

VI

The long argument I have given refutes the conventionalist claim that the name-inventor can have privileged knowledge of biconditional (I) in section III earlier by refuting the left-to-right conditional in (I). This is the more difficult refutation, and the philosophical questions raised are more interesting. It is easy enough to refute the claim that the name-inventor has privileged knowledge of the right-to-left conditional as well, though that demands a different scenario.

For instance, the namer tells others the name, and a planet is found in about the right place. For decades it is called 'Neptune'. Eventually a revolution in planetary mechanics takes place that makes it clear that the well-known, thoroughly explored planet Neptune cannot affect the orbits of any other planet. Coincidentally, a year later, a very small planet with various strange properties is observed for the first time. Given the new planetary mechanics, it is clear that *this* planet is causally responsible for the orbital perturbations previously blamed on Neptune. Somebody names it 'Diana', and once again everyone agrees that for years we were all wrong about the causal effects of Neptune. Even the great Leverrier, who gave it its name, was wrong.

Here again, no matter how thoroughly a priori and incorrigible Leverrier's knowledge of his mental acts of naming may be, and no matter how fervently he forms the intention always to use the name 'Neptune' in *his* idiolect according to certain rules, his intention *may* not be realized, the name *may* be handled in the public language as I just described, and he *may* turn out wrong about (I) because he is wrong about the right-to-left conditional in (I). He can be *very sure* my scenario will never take place, but he can only be sure on empirical grounds. Another retreat into privacy of referential standards will fail again.

VII

In summary, by accepting enough Cartesian epistemology of the mental, and by considering only acts of naming that are pure mental acts, we can get the result that a name-introducer has privileged access to the fact that he has introduced a name. But we *cannot* move from this position to the much stronger position that a name-introducer has epistemological privileges with respect to extramental facts, such as the biconditional (I). In fact, since the kind of shift in beliefs I described in my little scenario could happen in any case whatever, there is good reason to think it is false that name-introducers ever have such privileges.

Notes

I am indebted to Nuel Belnap, Richmond Thomason, Nathan Salmon and Joseph Camp for helpful criticisms of earlier versions of this essay.

1. The closest thing to an exception is Hilary Putnam's discussion in "The Analytic and the Synthetic," in *Philosophical Papers*, vol. 2, *Mind, Language and Reality* (Cambridge: Cambridge University Press, 1975).

2. Gerald J. Massey, "Is 'Congruence' a Peculiar Predicate?" in *Boston Studies in the Philosophy of Science*, vol. 8, ed. R. S. Cohen and R. C. Buck (Dordrecht: Reidel, 1971), 606–615.

3. Saul Kripke, "Naming and Necessity," in *Semantics of Natural Language*, Synthese Library, vol. 40, ed. Donald Davidson and Gilbert Harman (Dordrecht: Reidel, 1972), 347–348.

4. Kripke nowhere explicitly separates claim (i) from claim (ii). That he would accept both is apparent from discussions in Kripke, "Naming and Necessity," especially 274–275 and 347–348.

5

NEWCOMB'S PROBLEM AS
A THOUGHT EXPERIMENT

Some philosophers believe that Newcomb's problem is a useful source of intuitions against which to test theories of rational choice. And some philosophers believe that Newcomb's problem is outrageous enough that intuitions about what to do in the face of it ought to have no bearing on the enterprise of codifying the principles of practical reason. I shall argue that if Newcomb's problem is considered properly, both of these opinions are right. Newcomb's problem, as ordinarily presented, conceals two very different kinds of philosophical thought experiment. One of them is a clear illustration of the importance of indirect strategies. The other is a thought experiment with interesting implications for metaphysics, but no relevance at all to the theory of rational choice.

I

An important part of the methodology of decision theory is testing principles of rational choice by performing thought experiments. Performing a thought experiment in this field consists in constructing a hypothetical situation in which someone is faced with a decision, seeing what decision intuitively seems rational, and comparing this decision to the one yielded by the principles of decision endorsed by some theory. This methodology, like any other scientific methodology, raises certain questions. What conditions, if any, must a hypothetical situation meet in order to be relevant as a test case for a theory of rational choice? Are there systematic errors one should be aware of when testing theories in this way? By focusing on a case where this methodology has not resulted in smooth sailing, I hope to shed some light on these methodological issues.

The central point to notice in attacking these two questions is that it is impossible to describe the hypothetical decision situation without building into the description a great many normative facts. Otherwise, the people described will be mere shadows of people. The normative facts that are relevant here are epistemic. For instance, agents may be described as assigning certain subjective probabilities to certain propositions, or as having (or lacking) good reason for certain beliefs, or as knowing certain propositions and not others.

The normative facts can be included in two different ways. We can describe the people in great detail; we can describe their epistemic standards, their psychology, and all their evidence. Good novelists can do this well. Philosophers are typically less skilled at it, and, more importantly, philosophers must bring out very sharply the normative facts that are especially relevant to the purpose of the thought experiment. The other way to include the normative facts is to stipulate them.

When the normative facts of a hypothetical situation are stipulated to some extent, I will call the thought experiment a "schema." In one commonly used example, one stipulates that people in a certain hypothetical situation *know* that there is a gene that both inclines people to smoke cigarettes and disposes them to contract lung cancer. A "realization" of this schema is the result of filling out the description of the hypothetical people in a way that makes one or more stipulated normative facts become a plausible interpretation of the people's evaluative position in the hypothetical situation. For instance, one could describe the sort of evidence people have for a hypothesis about genes, smoking, and cancer, and describe the scientific sophistication of the people, thereby making it plausible to interpret them as knowing "there is a gene that...." A realization of a thought experiment is any such "filling in" of a thought experiment schema. Obviously a schema can be more or less filled in; thus the term "realization" is convenient shorthand for more precise but unnecessary relational terminology. Usually there will be different realizations of a given schema.

When a thought experiment schema is realized, we may discover that the particular realization requires us to drop some stipulated normative fact other than the one that we have "realized away." We may even discover, upon making a number of tries at realization, that we cannot realize the schematic thought experiment at all without invalidating some of the stipulated normative facts. This would happen if we started with a thought-experiment schema concerning a "completely moral ax-murderer" in a culture essentially like ours. Nobody would be taken in by such a case. But in more interesting cases, the risk of making normative stipulations that will not survive realization is real. And in interesting cases, there is always the risk that staying at the level of stipulation of a given thought experiment schema will blind us to the variety of realizations. This has happened with Newcomb's problem.

"Newcomb's problem" asks what we should do if the following events took place: A mysterious extraterrestrial being descends and astounds us for a while with various exhibitions of inhuman intellectual prowess. As a curtain-closing act, the being leaves a pair of boxes for each adult human, one transparent and containing a thousand dollars and one opaque. The being announces that it has predicted what each of us will do when, as has been scheduled, we choose to take either the contents of both boxes or the contents only of the opaque box. On the basis of these predictions, the being has placed a million dollars in someone's opaque box if the person will choose just that box, and nothing in the opaque box if the person will choose both boxes. As time goes by, many thousands of people make choices, and the being's rate of successful prediction is very high, around 90 percent (about nine of ten one-boxers have found a million, and nine of ten two-boxers have found only the obvious thousand). "Our" time has come to choose.

The Newcomb problem stipulates that (I) we know that a superior being has made predictions about our choices far into the future and arranged money in boxes accordingly. It also stipulates that (II) we know a fair amount about the outcome of people making their choices but (III) we do not understand the causal processes that lead to these outcomes. I will argue that there is no way to realize the three stipulations of this thought experiment schema while at the same time having a thought experiment that is relevant to the theory of rational choice.

II

I shall use the term "causal decision theory" for the following variation on classical Bayesian decision theory.[1]

Suppose an agent must choose among alternative actions $A_1, \ldots, A_n$. And suppose that the agent has a way of partitioning the world into a set of logically exhaustive and logically mutually exclusive possible states $S_1, \ldots, S_m$. For each alternative action A_i and possible state S_j, the action will result in an "outcome" O_{ij}. Assume the agent has, and recognizes, preferences among these outcomes in a way that can be codified by assigning a numerical utility value to each outcome. Finally, the agent knows his subjective probabilities for each conditional of the form "If I perform A_i, then O_{ij} will obtain." These conditionals have as truth conditions the requirement that "If I perform A, then B will obtain" is true if and only if either my performing A brings about B, or B would obtain whether or not I performed A. Then the agent should proceed to assign an expected utility to each alternative action A_i by multiplying the probability of "If I perform A_i, then O_{ij} will obtain" by the utility value of O_{ij}, and adding these results for each j.[2] If some action A_i receives the highest expected utility, the agent should perform it.

"Bayesian decision theory" replaces the probability of the conditional "If I perform A_i, then O_{ij} will occur" by the conditional probability of O_{ij} on A_i.

I shall use the term "the dominance principle" for the decision rule that says that an agent should perform an action that weakly dominates its alternatives. Action A_i weakly dominates the rest of $A_1 \ldots A_n$ if and only if for some set of possible states $S_1 \ldots S_m$, logically exhaustive, logically mutually exclusive and causally independent of $A_1 \ldots A_n$, the outcome of A_i in some possible state S_j is preferred by the agent to the outcomes in S_j of all other actions in the set $A_1 \ldots A_n$, and in no possible state is the outcome of any other action preferred to the outcome of A_i in that possible state.

Some philosophers believe that in the circumstances described by Newcomb's problem, we would find the dominance principle and Bayesian decision theory at odds in their recommendations while causal decision theory would make the same recommendation as the dominance principle (which, moreover, is intuitively right).[3] I will argue that this would constitute partial grounds for accepting causal decision theory *only* if the situation of Newcomb's problem is a choice situation we could in principle confront.

I shall argue later that there is a realization of Newcomb's problem that seems to be the problem these philosophers have in mind, but that falls short of doing what it is supposed to do, since it is not a choice situation that we could confront. First I shall consider another realization of Newcomb's problem. Realized in this way, it is a thought experiment that describes a situation that we could in principle confront, and it provides intuitive data useful in an investigation of decision theory. It does not, however, support causal decision theory against Bayesian decision theory. (Of course, other thought experiments may do so.)

III

Consider the following realization of Newcomb's problem. The question is this: Suppose we have good reason to think an extraterrestrial being has visited us for a while. (I stipulate as a constraint on the hypothetical situation that we have good reason, of whatever kind, for believing that this was an extraterrestrial). Moreover, we have some evidence that the Being performed remarkable feats of prediction. For instance, the being seems to have announced days or weeks ahead of time what certain people would do or say on some occasion. Most of these announcements turned out in retrospect to have been true, so far as "we" can tell. Perhaps the results have been reported in the news media, and confirmed in one or two cases by observers "we" know personally. Further, we have good reason to believe the being announced before leaving that boxes were going to be left for each of us, with money distributed in the boxes on the basis of predictions made by the being (details as usual). Finally, we have good reason to believe that nine out of ten one-boxers so far have found a million, while nine out of ten two-boxers have found empty opaque boxes. What should we do?

Presumably all attempts to explain how the being could manage such incredible predictions have been unconvincing. We have no idea how anyone or anything could do it. But we all know there are hustlers. It is far more reasonable to believe in an extraterrestrial hustler than to believe in an extraterrestrial seer capable of predicting years or even months ahead the outcome of individual human decisions. (An exception: If nearly everyone had been, say, a one-boxer, we would have some reason to believe that this reflects a surprising regularity in human behavior which might somehow have been antecedently known.) The being, probably together with whatever humans are involved in the enterprise of placing and guarding boxes, supervising choices, and so on, cheats. Either the distribution of money is triggered by the physical act of selecting boxes, or it is triggered somewhat earlier by tip-off behavior exhibited by people about to choose.

Of course, we will know that many people seem to believe in the prediction myth, but people can be taken in rather easily by simple, human conjuring or mind-reading trickery. If we are reasonable people, and we want to know in detail why the being's supposed "predictions" have been so "accurate," we should hope that the matter will be investigated by people competent to uncover conspiracies, detect the use of conjurers' apparatus, recognize mentalists' techniques, or contribute in some other way to uncovering large-scale fraud.

No reasonable person would think otherwise in this situation. And no additional details of the case will affect this conclusion. (For instance, suppose we learn that the box-tenders were not selected by the being. They are randomly chosen West Point cadets. Reply: It is far more reasonable to believe West Point cadets can be bribed than to believe that some creature can predict free human behavior years in advance). Of course, Newcomb's problem, as ordinarily presented, simply stipulates that we know the being has left money according to its predictions. But in the quite well-defined hypothetical situation I have described, we would not know any such thing. Stipulation (I) cannot be sustained, given the epistemic position we would actually find ourselves in.

Deciding what to do in this realization of the Newcomb problem would amount to deciding whether there seemed to be a way to beat the system. We can imagine variations on the problem where there is. Investigation by qualified people might show that the distribution of money is triggered by the actual behavior of box selection. Perhaps selections are announced in the hall outside the box room, whereupon giggling box-tenders go in and "bring out the contents of" the selected boxes. It would be clear that they reward one-boxers most of the time, so we should take one box. This is not an interesting subcase.

The following is an interesting subcase. Physical selection of boxes is done by going alone into a room in which the boxes rest in plain view on an open table. The selection process is filmed by what seems to be an ordinary automatic movie camera, supposedly to prevent cheating by the person making the selection. (All of this is reported in the media and also by several generally reliable friends who have made their selections.)

Before going in to make a selection, the candidate is interviewed for an hour by box-tenders.

Here it would be reasonable to think the box-tenders attempt to discover during the interview what the candidate will do, and succeed about nine times out of ten. They plant the money accordingly. There would be some probability that the physical act of selection triggers some very sophisticated apparatus that very rapidly affects an unobserved distribution of money. But there would be a much higher probability that during the prechoice interview the interviewers decide what the candidate will do, and arrange the money before the physical act of box-selection occurs. Further details of the standard interview might or might not give us clues as to what the tip-offs are that the interviewers look for. If the interviewers typically stuck to asking general personal questions while studiously watching the candidate, it would seem they used some kind of "cold-reading" technique, the disciplined practical psychology that has long been an art form among professional fortune tellers. In that case, we would be hard put to guess which behaviors of ours would be salient. On the other hand, the interviewers might be more transparent. For instance, they might frequently and unexpectedly ask, "How many boxes will you take," looking at stopwatches to measure the response time. In this case, we could make speculative conjectures about their diagnostic method, but surely not with much confidence.

I shall assume these details can be filled in so as to make it plausible that we would be in the following epistemic position: (a) The probability is very high that behavior people exhibit during the interview tips off the interviewers what choice will be made, and the money is suitably arranged sometime before the physical act of box-selection. (b) The probability is very low that the trick is done by some mechanism that injects or removes money as a causal result of physical box-selection. (c) No hypothesis about the diagnostic methods of the interviewers is reasonable enough and detailed enough to justify the risk of trying to beat them at their game by faking just a few selected tip-off behaviors during the interview.

Our problem would be to behave as nearly as we can the way "typical" one-boxers behave during the interview. We might come up with a clever trick enabling us to do this, but actually take both boxes. Perhaps we could have ourselves hypnotized and given a complicated suggestion requiring us to "believe" we were going to take one box up to the last second, and then switch. We would need to have a great deal of confidence in this approach to justify the risk, and I shall consider only the case where we do not have such confidence.

The reasonable strategy for us to adopt would be an "indirect strategy." In my terminology, an indirect strategy for achieving an end involves setting oneself, or developing a firm intention, to perform an action A not because one thinks it probable that A itself will cause the desired end, but because one thinks it probable that something or other that one will do (perhaps unknowingly) as a result of having the intention to perform A will cause the desired end. When these conditions are satisfied, I say that it is probable that action A will "bring about" the desired end.

Indirect strategies of a slightly different kind are available when the action is a long-term practice. It can be probable that one will achieve a desired end by engaging in long-term practice A because it is probable that something or other one does in the course of this practice causes the end. For instance, it might be a good indirect strategy, in this sense, to form oneself, or one's child, as an altruist so as to maximize one's own possible sources of pleasure by enabling oneself to take pleasure in the well-being of others.

A simpler example would be a situation where we know there is a strong statistical correlation between cigarette smoking and lung cancer, but where we also have expert scientific opinion that nothing in the smoke of cigarettes is carcinogenic. Various hypotheses would be available, including the hypothesis that the scientific opinion is wrong, and the hypothesis that some causal factors lead to a coincidence of cigarette smoking and a carcinogenic environment (or even a coincidence of cigarette smoking and a carcinogenic life-style). For instance, commercial advertising and social customs that encourage smoking also encourage smoking in bars. Drinking alcohol might directly cause a cancer liability, or, more treacherously, something about bars might be carcinogenic (think of it as a carcinogenic fungus found largely in bars). In ignorance of the correct hypothesis, but strongly preferring no smoking and no cancer to smoking and cancer, a good indirect strategy would be to stop smoking.

In the realization of Newcomb's problem I have described, an indirect strategy of the first kind is in order. In fact, the problem is a clear illustration of the rationality of such strategies. The reasonable thing to do is form the firm intention of taking one box and stick to it. It is foolish to attempt an end run around accomplished tricksters who know their trickery as well as three-card monte hustlers know theirs. The suggestion might be made that we mimic the effect of the hypnotic suggestion scenario by sheer cleverness, first pretending to intend taking just one box, but finally snatching both. If there were evidence that others had tried such a ploy successfully, it might be reasonable. But in the absence of such evidence, we should consider the usual fate of marks like us who try outfoxing a skilled mentalist and the powerful evidence that these box-tenders are skilled mentalists although they do not say so. We want to make them think we are one-boxers, but we do not know how to do this except by being one-boxers. There is another possibility, of course. It might be that at the interview, the box-tenders psycho-logically manipulate candidates into making a particular choice (in con-jurers' jargon, they "force" a given choice). We cannot do anything about that, and must ignore this possibility in deliberation about a supposedly free choice.

Whenever we try to use an indirect strategy to achieve some end, we should realize that the point of the strategy is to ensure that we perform some action or other that will be efficacious in securing the end, although we may not be able to conceptually individuate the action in a way that would enable us to directly undertake to perform it. In the case at hand, we can say that we must "appear to be prospective one-boxers to the interviewers" but we do not know what act-types at other levels of description will make us so appear. Our total evidence makes it very probable that if we steadfastly set ourselves to take one box, some pattern of behavior we engage in will result ultimately in there being a million dollars in the opaque box. We can call that pattern of behavior "action X," in which case what we want to do is to perform action X. The action "taking one box" is explicitly cited in our formulation of the indirect strategy, whereas action X is not. But this should not make us think that we are deciding to perform the action "taking one box" *simpliciter*. We are deciding to perform action X by means of a strategy that requires us, among other things, to take one box.

Looked at this way, our decision turns on whether to perform action X by means of the strategy of firmly and constantly intending to take one box. Let A_1, be taking one box, A_2 be taking two boxes, m be the state of there being a million in the opaque box, $-m$ be the state of there being nothing in the opaque box, XA_1 be performing action X by firmly and constantly intending to perform A_1, and let A_3 be some live alternative, such as using hypnosis to enable us to appear as one-boxers but switch at the last moment (nothing is affected by simplifying our position to one where this is the only live alternative). Then Bayesian decision theory requires us to assess the conditional probability of m and $-m$ on XA_1 and A_2. The subjective probabilities of m on XA_1 and $-m$ on A_2 are high, whereas the probabilities of $-m$ on XA_1 and m on A_2 are low. Bayesian decision theory recommends XA_1 against A_2. (I assume the reader can supply enough details of the case to justify numbers that work.)

Causal decision theory requires us to assess the subjective probability of the conditionals:

(i) If I perform XA_1 then m will occur.
(ii) If I perform XA_1 then $-m$ will occur.
(iii) If I perform A_2 then m will occur.
(iv) If I perform A_2 then $-m$ will occur.

(i) and (iv) are very probable, while (ii) and (iii) are improbable. Causal decision theory recommends XA_1 against A_2.

The dominance principle cannot be applied, since the condition that m and $-m$ be causally independent of XA_1 and A_2 is not known by us to be satisfied. It is very probable that it is not satisfied, but we do not know this for certain. So in this realization of Newcomb's problem, both Bayesian and causal decision theory recommend the same decision, and neither is inconsistent with dominance reasoning.

It might be argued that if we try to compare the acts A_1 and A_2, rather than XA_1 and A_2, causal decision theory recommends the wrong action. The argument goes like this: A_1 is the correct choice over against A_2, since doing A_1 is required by a correct indirect strategy. But it is extremely likely in this hypothetical situation that the money will be distributed before either A_1 or A_2 is actually performed. So causal decision theory recommends performing A_2. The modification this argument forces in causal decision theory is minor. We need only understand "brings about" in the truth conditions for the conditionals in the way I defined it in section III, earlier, rather than as equivalent to "causes."

IV

The realization of Newcomb's problem discussed in the previous section fills in enough details concerning the epistemic position of the people who appear in the thought experiment to justify interpreting them as satisfying stipulations (II) and (III). But this realization requires dropping stipulation (I). I have suggested that there is some modest philosophical payoff from considering this realization. Since it is a realization in which the people are epistemically like us, it reflects what we would actually think and do if we were confronted with the claims that constitute Newcomb's problem together with the sort of evidence for those claims usually envisaged by writers on the subject. I tailored the final details so as to make up a useful thought experiment that illustrates the rationality of indirect strategies (of one kind) and that lets us see how Bayesian and causal decision theory should be brought to bear in such cases. Clearly, our theories of rational choice can be fairly tested by this thought experiment. It concerns a situation that we could confront, and a theory of rational choice should recommend the correct action in any such situation where it applies at all.

It might be thought that this realization of Newcomb's problem is not the most interesting one. It is stipulation (I) that has especially gripped philosophers studying the problem. Even if the realization with people most like us forces us to abandon stipulation (I), we must allow some other realization that preserves it. We can describe a second realization in which (I) is preserved, but at great cost to its utility as a thought experiment in decision theory. Suppose we want to preserve the stipulation that we know the being has predicted what we will do and long ago distributed money accordingly. This requires that "we" be very different from the way we are culturally. It is better to imagine a civilization of people for whom it would be rational to accept, even after careful discussion and reflection, that the being had a way to make months-or-years-ahead predictions of human decisions, rather than rejecting this in favor of the hypothesis of an elaborate deception. Call them the Gullibles.

The Gullibles must be unlike us in deep ways. One of us who endorsed the predicting-being hypothesis would do so in the face of (ignored) epistemically relevant experience of human nature: experience of human deceit and conspiracy on the one hand, and experience of the unpredictability of human behavior over long stretches of time on the other hand. One of *us* who did that would not be a Gullible. He would be an epistemically inconsistent person who assigned probabilities out of line with available evidence. We want to imagine true Gullibles, people who can assign a high probability to the predicting-being hypothesis consistently with their other assignments of subjective probability.

One way to do this is to suppose that the Gullibles don't have the concepts of fraud and deception, and are thus unable to frame the hypothesis that there is trickery and fraudulent misrepresentation in the Newcomb problem. I prefer another picture of them, one that maximizes similarities between them and at least some of us: Assume the Gullibles believe people sometimes have magical powers enabling them to see the future. The Gullibles also have concepts of fraud and trickery, but these concepts are narrower than ours. In the Gullible worldview, a person can "trick" another by seducing him into doing something, for example, by making a false promise. But the Gullibles do not believe people can substantially manipulate the apparent causal order of nature. Certain itinerant gypsies among them perform card tricks and work elaborate confidence games with deceptive props, but Gullible conventional wisdom has it that these gypsies are magical seers. Gullible scientific psychology has evolved several imaginative theories of prescience, although hard-nosed critics among them question whether these theories are robustly testable.

Suppose someone goes up to a Gullible and claims to be able to predict by looking into the future what card the Gullible will randomly select from a deck. He writes something on a piece of paper, seals it in an envelope, and hands the Gullible a deck of 52 cards, each of which is a queen of spades. The Gullible chooses a card without looking at the faces. The paper turns out to say "queen of spades." Presumably, the Gullible will take this as good, although perhaps not absolutely conclusive, evidence that the other person predicted an essentially random event by seeing the future. But, what is more important, the Gullible will do this without further inquiry and without supposing that further inquiry might be in order. He would not bother to turn over the cards because he will not have a likely enough alternative hypothesis (except "it was luck," and that could be taken care of by further trials).

Gullibles would not, as we would, assign a low probability to prescience in card magic pending further investigation for fakery. This is a principled difference in the way they make epistemic evaluations, and it would affect a great many judgments. When people claim to know that something will happen later, it is uncommon for us to investigate for fraud and deception. But this is either because little hangs on it, or because we have "trust" of a certain kind. Gullibles would not investigate for fraud and deception of this kind no matter what hung on it, and they would have no need for our concept of trust, recognizing nothing of significant practical importance to contrast it with. Thus the Gullibles will respond to Newcomb-problem evidence by endorsing the predicting-being hypothesis. They don't think at all likely, or even see, possibilities that we see and that we consider significant. They accept as live possibilities things that we rule out as absurd. These differences make for the differences in the assignment of prior probabilities brought by the Gullibles into the Newcomb problem.

A true Gullible is not like you and me, however gullible we may sometimes be through epistemic inconsistency. We would not and could not become Gullibles as a result of certain new experiences, not even as a result of watching a large silver sphere land in the back yard, followed by weeks of hearing and reading about so-called astounding predictions. No such experience could blot out the experience of the world, including people, we have already accumulated. We could "become Gullibles" by gradual cultural evolution, and we could have been raised in a Gullible culture in the first place. But we cannot become Gullibles as a result of confronting a novel situation and gathering information about it.

Let us consider, then, a realization of the schematic Newcomb problem in which "we" may be plausibly interpreted as rationally accepting the predicting-being hypothesis, so that if it is true we could argue that we know it, as stipulated in the schema (I)–(III). This realization (hereafter "the second") requires that we be Gullibles. Therefore, *we* cannot confront such a situation, in the sense of "cannot" described earlier. I suggest that theories of rational decision need only stand testing in hypothetical situations that *we* can confront, in this sense of "can." Otherwise, we shall have to demand that such theories reflect the "rational" decision that would, intuitively, be made by people whose cultural epistemic standards are substantially unlike ours. This would be like demanding that moral theories survive testing in thought experiments about cultures where unhappiness is prized or social discord positively sought.

A natural reply is that if we consider sufficiently high-level epistemic standards, we would see that the Gullibles need not differ from us. For instance, they, like us, are guided by the rule: Before accepting an explanation, investigate whether alternative explanations better fit the facts. It is just that in some cases they don't see serious alternatives where we do. But all sorts of epistemic standards, high-level and low-level, will come into play in a given decision situation, and epistemic standards at this level of generality are compatible with all sorts of outlandish lower level standards, for instance, taking statistical data that can be interpreted as showing retro-causation as very probably indicating retro-causation. We would not expect a good theory of rational choice to imply and legitimate the decisions deemed rational by people who thought like this. Analogously, people who prize unhappiness might still coincide with us in moral standards at a high level of generality, such as "seek to maximize what is prized." Moral theories should not be tested against the moral judgments of such people as these.

The second realization of the Newcomb problem is intelligible. Unlike the first, it cashes in stipulation (I) in the schema of the New-comb problem. And also unlike the first, it is a thought experiment irrelevant to decision theory.

A final remark: If no realization of a given thought experiment schema is evidence for one philosophical theory against another, then the thought experiment schema does not decide between these theories. Plausibly, the realizations of Newcomb's problem I have described exhaust the interesting possibilities. So, plausibly, Newcomb's problem provides no evidence for causal decision theory *vis-à-vis* Bayesian decision theory.

Notes

I am indebted to Joseph Camp, John Forge, Richard Jeffrey, Gerald Massey, and Nicholas Rescher for helpful criticisms of earlier versions of this essay.

1. Versions of causal decision theory can be found in David Lewis, "Causal Decision Theory," *Australasian Journal of Philosophy* 59 (1981), 5–30. Allan Gibbard and William Harper, "Counterfactuals and Two Kinds of Expected Utility," in *Foundations and Applications of Decision Theory*, vol. 1, ed. C. A. Hooker, J. J. Leach, and E. F. McClennan (Dordrecht: Reidel, 1978), 125–162. Brian Skyrms, "The Role of Causal Factors in Rational Decision," in *Causal Necessity* (New Haven:

Yale University Press, 1980), 128–139. The version I describe is essentially that of Gibbard and Harper.

2. The semantics for these conditionals is stipulated. The reader can translate them into the subjunctive if that seems preferable.

3. For example, see Gibbard and Harper, "Counterfactuals," 153.

6

PHILOSOPHICAL INTUITIONS
AND PSYCHOLOGICAL THEORY

I

Some philosophers, particularly ethicists and epistemologists, see as one of their tasks the discovery of norms, ethical or epistemological, that we more or less live by. Reflection on naturally occurring moral or epistemological dilemmas will reveal these norms to some extent, just as observation of the physical world will reveal the laws of physics to some extent. But just as physicists must perform controlled experiments to decide among rival hypotheses that they cannot distinguish by observing naturally occurring events, philosophers must perform thought experiments to illuminate norms that naturally occurring dilemmas don't reveal. This is not to say that ethics is like physics in other respects. Physicists see themselves as discovering physical laws, whereas philosophers often take themselves to be exploring the structure of our concepts, or, in the case of ethicists, uncovering moral norms.

It is an open question to what extent philosophical thought experiments can reveal norms. Only case studies can answer the question or at least answer it in part. This article is such a case study.

II

Warren Quinn relies on thought experiments in his discussion of what he calls the "Doctrine of Doing and Allowing." He writes:

Sometimes we cannot benefit one person without harming, or failing to help, another; and where the cost to the other would be serious—where, for example, he would die—a substantial moral question is

168

raised: would the benefit justify the harm? Some moralists would answer this question by balancing the good against the evil. But others deny that consequences are the only things of moral relevance. To them it matters whether the harm comes from action, for example from killing someone, or from inaction, for example from not saving someone. They hold that for some good ends we may properly allow some evil to befall someone, even though we could not actively bring that evil about.[1]

The proposition expressed by the last sentence of this passage is the Doctrine of Doing and Allowing. Quinn appeals to philosophical thought experiments for three distinct, though related, reasons. First, he tries to refine the Doctrine of Doing and Allowing by testing various formulations of it against intuitions that naturally arise when one performs various thought experiments. Second, he appeals to the intuitions one has while performing certain thought experiments as grounds for accepting the Doctrine of Doing and Allowing. Third, he argues that these intuitions show that the ethical norms at work in these cases should not be given a consequentialist analysis. The following thought experiment is typical; in fact, this is the only one of Quinn's thought experiments I shall consider in this article. I believe there will be no loss of generality.

The thought experiment:

Choose the appropriate action in each of the following two cases.
Rescue Dilemma 1: We can either save five people in danger of drowning in one place or a single person in danger of drowning somewhere else. We cannot save all six.
Rescue Dilemma 2: We can save the five only by driving over and thereby killing someone who (for an unspecified reason) is trapped on the road. If we do not undertake the rescue, the trapped person can later be freed.[2]

Quinn's intuition is that in Rescue Dilemma 1 we are perfectly justified in saving the group of five people, even though we thereby fail to save the solitary person, whereas in Rescue Dilemma 2 it is "far from obvious that we *may* proceed."[3] In his discussion, he reports that the intuitions of some other philosophers match his own. And he seems to think it likely that the reader will have intuitions that match his own. For the purposes of this article, I shall assume that Quinn is right about this widespread similarity of intuitions.

Quinn appears to assume that anyone who responds to these cases as he does has moral intuitions, which, like his, conform to the Doctrine of Doing and Allowing. After trying several formulations of this doctrine, he writes: "Perhaps we have found the basic form of the doctrine and the natural qualifications that, when combined with other plausible moral principles, accurately map our moral intuitions."[4] Quinn then goes on to develop a philosophical defense of the doctrine. I am not concerned here with whether or not there is a philosophical defense of the Doctrine of Doing and Allowing. I am concerned instead with Quinn's assumption that people who share his intuitions in the case of Rescue Dilemma 1 and Rescue Dilemma 2 do so because they accept, however inexplicitly, the Doctrine of Doing and Allowing. Indeed, I am concerned with Quinn's assumption that he himself has these intuitions because he (antecedently) accepts the Doctrine of Doing and Allowing. The ground for my concern is that it might be the case, rather, that Quinn has these intuitions as a result of covert reasoning of the kind posited by prospect theory. If this is the best explanation, then Quinn is wrong to think of these intuitions as the product of a very different pattern of reasoning involving a distinction between doing and allowing.

III

Daniel Kahneman and Amos Tversky developed prospect theory to be a descriptive theory of human decision making which would match the decisions people actually make better than classical expected utility theory would.[5] For instance, prospect theory predicts the following experimental results, whereas classical expected utility theory does not.

The subjects in one group were given the following decision problem:

Assume yourself richer by $300 than you are today. You have to choose between:
    1. a sure gain of $100
and
    2. a 50 percent chance of gaining $200 and a 50 percent chance of gaining nothing.

The subjects in a second group were given this decision problem:

Assume yourself richer by $500 than you are today. You have to choose between:

1. a sure loss of $100

and

2. a 50 percent chance of losing nothing and a 50 percent chance
   of losing $200.

In problem 1, a majority of people chose the option that offers a sure gain rather than the risky option. In problem 2, a majority of people chose the risky option rather than the sure loss. So most people are risk averse in problem 1 and risk seeking in problem 2, despite the fact that in each case the decision maker faces a choice between gaining $400 for sure and an even chance of gaining $500 or gaining $300.[6] If people always acted so as to maximize expected utility, they would not exhibit this pattern of choices.[7]

In a second experiment, Kahneman and Tversky presented one group of subjects with this decision problem:

Imagine that the United States is preparing for an outbreak of an unusual Asian disease which is expected to kill six hundred people. Two alternative programs to fight the disease, A and B, have been proposed. Assume that the exact scientific estimates of the consequences of the programs are as follows:

If program A is adopted, two hundred people will be saved. If program B is adopted, there is a one-third probability that six hundred people will be saved, and a two-thirds probability that no people will be saved.

Which program would you choose?

The subjects in a second group were given the same cover story with the following description of two different alternative programs, C and D:

If program C is adopted, four hundred people will die. If program D is adopted, there is a one-third probability that nobody will die and a two-thirds probability that six hundred will die.

Once again the subjects were asked which program they would choose. Programs A and C are equivalent from the point of view of expected survival as are programs B and D. Nevertheless, a majority of the first group of subjects chose program A over program B, while a majority of the second group of subjects chose program D over program C. So when the outcomes were stated in positive terms, "lives saved," subjects tended to be risk averse, whereas when the outcomes were stated in negative terms, "lives lost," subjects tended to be risk seeking.

Prospect theory is designed to explain these and many similar experimental results, as well as a range of structurally distinct experimental results that are apparently in conflict with expected utility theory. The theory distinguishes two phases in the choice process, the first of which is "editing." During this phase, the options are reformulated so as to simplify the second phase of the choice process, the evaluation of the prospects. The editing phase consists of a number of different operations, only one of which need concern us here: "framing."[8] In the framing process, the agent chooses one possible outcome of her actions as the "neutral" outcome. And she classifies the other possible outcomes as either "gains" or "losses" relative to this neutral outcome; that is, she classifies outcomes as either "positive" or "negative" deviations from the neutral outcome.

In the evaluation phase of the choice process, the agent rates each of the contemplated alternative actions. As is common in expected utility theory, possible alternative actions are conceived of as distributions of probability over outcomes. The idea is that for any given contemplated action, the agent expects various outcomes to follow upon her performing the action, where these levels of expectation can be expressed as a probability. During the evaluation phase, the agent encodes her judgments of desirability differences with a value function, v. The function v takes the value 0 for the neutral outcome and takes positive or negative real values for other outcomes in such a way as to reflect the positive or negative deviations in desirability of those outcomes from the neutral outcome. It is an open question as to what factors determine an agent's selection of a neutral outcome, although it often seems to correspond to the status quo. What is most important for my purposes, though, is that different formulations of a decision problem can lead an agent to make different choices of the neutral outcome. How this can happen will become clear when we turn to the prospect-theoretic analysis of the first experiment. But first let us complete our sketch of the theory.

In deciding which actions are preferable to which other actions, agents do not simply multiply the value of outcomes by the probability of those outcomes. Some probabilities are factored in at more than their face value, while other probabilities are factored in at less than their face value. Or so a large body of experimental research seems to suggest. To reflect this fact, prospect theory attributes to the agent a weighting function, $w(p)$, which associates with each probability a "decision weight."

Suppose the possible actions available to an agent are very simple in form. Each of them can be represented by a probability distribution $(x, p; y, q)$. A possible action, or "prospect," of the form $(x, p; y, q)$ is a possible action regarded by the agent as leading to outcome x with probability p and outcome y with probability q, and leading to the neutral outcome with probability $1 - p - q$. For the moment, assume that outcomes are monetary amounts. Prospects can be strictly positive, strictly negative, or regular. A prospect $(x, p; y, q)$ is strictly positive if $x > y > 0$ and $p + q = 1$, strictly negative if $x < 0$ and $y < 0$, and regular otherwise. The all-in value of the action $(x, p; y, q)$, in the eyes of this agent, is denoted in prospect theory by $D(x, p; y, q)$. If $(x, p; y, q)$ is a regular prospect, prospect theory proposes that $D(x, p; y, q)$ is equal to $w(p)v(x) + w(q)v(y)$, where $v(0) = 0$, $w(0) = 0$, and $w(1) = 1$. Clearly, D and v will coincide for sure prospects, since $D(x, 1.0) = v(x)$. Prospect theory suggests a different rule for evaluating positive and negative prospects, but that need not concern us here, since the prospects we will be considering are all regular.[9] The generalization to the case of an action with some finite number of possible outcomes greater than two follows the same pattern.

Many studies have confirmed that value functions over possible outcomes generally conform to the following pattern. They are concave for gains, convex for losses, and steeper for losses than for gains. People tend to be risk averse when it comes to gains, risk seeking when it comes to losses, and their response to losses tends to be more extreme than their response to gains.[10] In the first experiment, for example, prospect theory explains why people tend to prefer the sure gain to the risky alternative and disprefer the sure loss to the risky alternative, although the sure gain and the sure loss are equivalent in terms of expected monetary value, as are the two risky options.

The explanation goes like this: In the first part of the experiment, a typical subject picks the status quo plus $300 as the neutral outcome. The subject regards a further gain of $100 as a positive deviation from this neutral reference point, and she regards a further gain of $200 as an even greater positive deviation from the reference point. But she does not evaluate a gain of $200 as having twice the value of a gain of $100. This reflects the concavity of her v function for gains (see fig. 6.1).

We assume that the decision weight of a 50 percent chance is 0.5. Then, if the all-in value D of a sure gain of $100 is given by $D = v = k$,

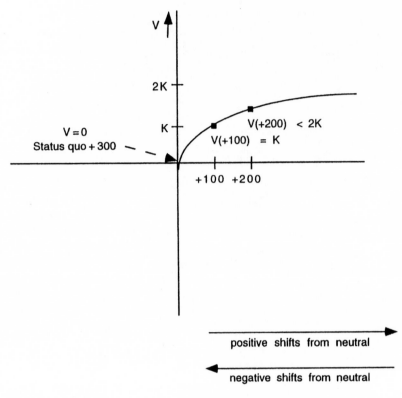

FIG. 6.1.

the subject will assign an all-in value less than *k* to the risky prospect, since she evaluates a gain of $200 at less than double a gain of $100.

In the second part of the experiment, a typical subject settles on the status quo plus $500 as the neutral reference point. She evaluates a loss of $100 and a loss of $200 as negative deviations from this reference point, but the value of her *v* function for a loss of $200 is not twice as large a negative as the value of her *v* function for a loss of $100. This reflects the convexity of *v* for losses (see fig. 6.2). As a result, the subject's all-in evaluation of a 50 percent chance of losing nothing and a 50 percent chance of losing $200 is greater than the subject's all-in evaluation of a sure loss of $100.

In this experiment, prospect theory yields a different prediction from expected utility theory for a combination of two reasons. First, differing instructions given to the subjects in the two parts of the experiment are assumed to result in differing choices of neutral reference point. Second,

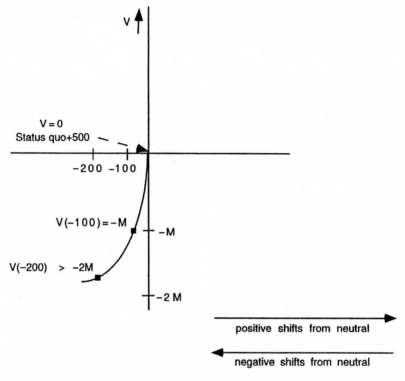

FIG. 6.2.

the valuation function for positive deviations from a reference point is assumed to be concave, whereas the valuation function for negative deviations from a reference point is assumed to be convex.

The prospect-theoretic analysis of the "Asian disease" experiment has exactly the same structure. The chief difference in this case is that it is assumed that subjects shift reference points because of the overall phrasing of the decision problem, not because some preliminary instruction of the form "assume you are x dollars richer than you are now" induces a choice of neutral outcome. In the first part of the experiment, for example, the results of disease-fighting programs are formulated in terms of "people saved." So one can hypothesize that subjects choose the outcome in which six hundred people are dead as the neutral outcome. But in the second part of the experiment, programs are described in terms of "people dying." So it is reasonable to assume that subjects choose the outcome in which six hundred people live as the

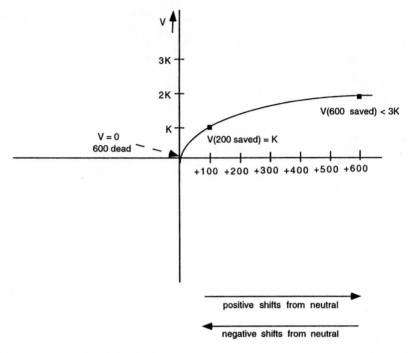

FIG. 6.3.

neutral reference point. As in the first experiment, this shift in neutral reference point presumably forces the subjects to evaluate disease-fighting programs as leading to positive deviations in one case but to negative deviations in the other, with a corresponding shift from concave to convex v functions (see figs. 6.3 and 6.4).

We must remember that prospect theory, as we have formulated it, hypothesizes that a certain psychological law characterizes these decision-making events and that the form of the law differs according to whether or not the possible actions involved are what are called 'regular prospects'. The definition of a 'regular prospect' presupposes that we are dealing with outcomes that have some natural numerical representation. This was plausible when the outcomes were monetary gains and losses. Perhaps it is equally plausible when the outcomes are human lives saved or human lives lost. Here our assumption has been that the natural numerical representation of such outcomes is determined by simply counting individual lives. But this is a substantive hypothesis about how

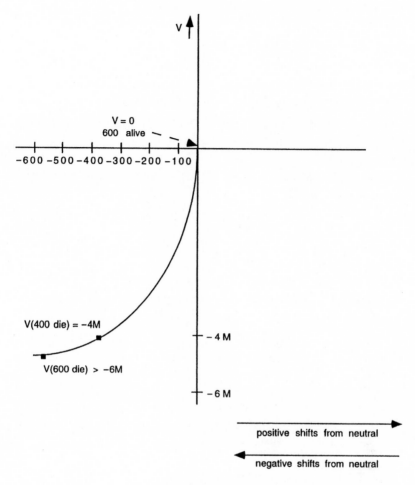

FIG. 6.4.

people measure the value of human life, and we have a right to wonder whether further empirical research would confirm the psychological reality of this simple numerical measure. It is worth noting, for instance, that some legislatures have decided to treat double murder as deserving the death penalty, when the murder of a single person, in the absence of other aggravating circumstances, deserves only life imprisonment. I only mean that remark to be suggestive. Perhaps, in some cases, we think of two deaths as much worse than one death. Nevertheless, for the remainder of this article, I will assume that it is psychologically realistic to suppose that people evaluate multiple deaths simply by body count.

IV

Now let us return to Quinn's thought experiment. Quinn assumes that he and others who share his intuitions respond differently to the first and second decision problems because they are sensitive to a difference between doing and allowing. But if we combine some of the basic insights of prospect theory with a few additional plausible assumptions, we can construct an alternative possible explanation for these same responses. Of course, in order to demonstrate that prospect theory offers a possible alternative explanation, these additional assumptions will have to be tested experimentally.

In the first rescue problem, Quinn expresses a preference for option 1 over option 2:

> *Option 1.*—*(a)* Save a group of five people in danger of drowning, and *(b)* fail to save one person in danger of drowning.
> *Option 2.*—*(c)* Save one person in danger of drowning, and *(d)* fail to save the group of five people in danger of drowning.

In considering the second rescue problem, however, Quinn is not sure how to rank option 3 relative to option 4:

> *Option 3.*—*(e)* Save a group of five people in danger of drowning, and *(f)* kill one person who would otherwise live.
> *Option 4.*—*(g)* Fail to save the group of five people in danger of drowning, and *(h)* refrain from killing one person.

The prospect-theoretic explanation of Quinn's intuitively clear ranking of options 1 and 2 versus his uncertainty in the case of options 3 and 4 can be developed in the following way. First, it is implicit in Quinn's discussion that choosing option 1 certainly will result in saving five lives and losing one life, choosing option 2 certainly will result in saving one life and losing five lives, and the other options have certain outcomes as well. Thus, the decision value D assigned by the decision-maker to these possible actions will be the outcome value v she has assigned to the outcome which has probability 1, as we saw earlier.

Our problem is to decide what outcome values Quinn is likely to be assigning to the various outcomes at issue in options 1 through 4. These outcomes are *(a)* and *(b)*, and *(c)* and *(d)* in the one case, and *(e)* and *(f)*, and *(g)* and *(h)* in the other. The best way to approach this problem is to consider a simpler example. You must decide what to do in each of two different decision problems. In the first problem, you must decide whether to kill someone who would otherwise be safe. In the second problem, you must decide whether to let someone die, even though you could save the person at no risk or cost to yourself. When you analyze these two problems, it may seem to you worse to kill than to let die. That is, it may seem to you that in the first problem, the reason you have to spare the person's life is more compelling than the reason you have to save the person in the second problem. This way of putting the matter presupposes that an agent can compare the force of the reasons for doing one thing or another across several distinct decision problems. Prospect theory does not contain this assumption, and it is problematic. It implies that an agent has evaluated the relevant outcomes in several different decision problems on the same scale. I doubt that this is true in general. But it may be true in some special circumstances, for example, when an agent is considering several decision problems that are very similar in structure and subject matter and when the agent is considering these problems at roughly the same time. That agents do compare the force of reasons in this way is an empirical hypothesis, and it should be tested. In the remainder of this article, I will assume that it is true.[11]

With this assumption in place, we can turn to prospect theory for an account of the differing intuitive responses between the two decision problems in this simple case. There is a shift in choice of neutral outcome. In deciding whether to kill the person or leave the person alone, one thinks of the person's being alive as the status quo and chooses this as the neutral outcome. Killing the person is regarded as a negative deviation, and its value is found in a correspondingly steep part of the v-curve. But in deciding whether to save a person who would otherwise die, one thinks of the person's being dead as the status quo and chooses this as the neutral outcome. So saving the person is a positive deviation, with a correspondingly less steep v-curve. Notice that here it is the comparative steepness of v-curves for positive versus negative deviations that does the explanatory work, not the concavity of one versus the convexity of the other (see figs. 6.5 and 6.6).

In the problem involving killing the person or letting the person live, the absolute value of v for the killing option is larger than the absolute value of v for the saving option in the problem involving saving or letting die. Or so we may assume, if it is legitimate to make this cross-problem comparison. So in the problem involving killing or letting live, the

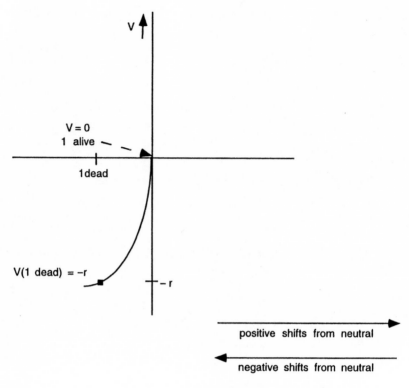

FIG. 6.5.

absolute value of D for the killing option is greater than the absolute value of D for the letting die option in the problem involving saving or letting die. Our conjecture is that this difference in the absolute value of D is perceived as a difference in the force of one's reasons in the two cases.

If this is right, then one's intuition that there is this difference in the force of the reasons should not be explained in terms of a perceived difference between action and inaction but rather in terms of differing responses to gains and to losses. The advantage of this explanation is that it rests on a psychological theory that predicts fairly well in a wide variety of decision-making situations. It is not clear that a theory that is based on perceived differences between action and inaction can be formulated with comparable empirical authority. Certainly none with comparable generality.

In order to go on to develop a prospect-theoretic account of the conjunctive acts in Quinn's original example, another assumption is needed. Quinn's Rescue Dilemma 1 and Rescue Dilemma 2 each

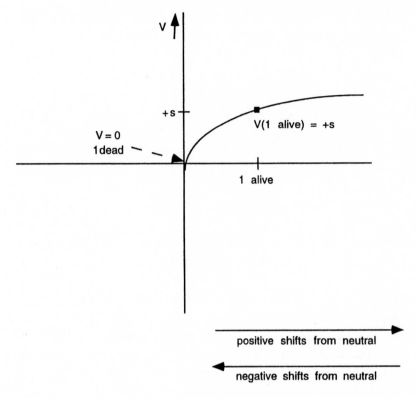

FIG. 6.6.

involve a comparison of conjunctive actions, that is, actions which lead with certainty to a conjunction of two outcomes. In Rescue Dilemma 1, the comparison is between actions in the forms of "do M and do X" and "do N and do Y." In Rescue Dilemma 2, the comparison is between actions in the forms of "do M and do F" and "do N and do G." The comparison of doing M with doing N is present in both problems.

The simplest assumption I can think of to deal with the valuation of actions with conjunctive outcomes is this: the agent separates the conjunctive outcome of each conjunctive action into its conjuncts, assigns a value of v to each conjunct, and adds these values of v to get a value of v for the conjunction of outcomes. In the cases we are considering, prospect theory would predict a value of D equal to the value of v for each conjunctive action. Now consider Rescue Dilemma 1. According to our assumption, the subject evaluates option 1 by adding the values of (a) and (b) taken separately. Likewise the subject evaluates option 2 by adding the values of (c) and (d) taken separately. The subject proceeds in the same way with Rescue Dilemma 2. It is clear that the absolute value of the difference in v for option 1 and option 2 will be larger than the absolute value of the difference in v for option 3 and option 4. This is because, in this case, just as in the simplified pair of decision problems I considered earlier, the gap in v between killing and sparing is larger than the gap in v between letting die and saving. Then, applying the first assumption, the subject perceives her reason for choosing option 1 over option 2 to be more compelling than her reason for choosing option 3 over option 4.

My simple assumption about the evaluation of conjunctions almost certainly is not generally valid. One would expect the conjuncts to interact to some degree, sometimes more and sometimes less. In the case of Quinn's Rescue Dilemmas, however, the interaction, if it exists, may be rather similar, between option 1 and option 3, and between option 2 and option 4. If this is so, our extension of prospect theory to this case should be approximately correct. It is obvious that this is an empirical hypothesis that must be tested. But with this assumption, as with our earlier assumption about cross-problem comparisons, we know what hypotheses about human psychology need to be tested in order for our philosophical analysis to succeed. With Quinn's proposal that the differences lie in differing evaluations of action and inaction, we do not know even this much.

Let us take stock of the epistemology of the situation. Quinn's intuitions can be explained fairly well by prospect theory. Prospect theory also explains subjects' intuitions in many other kinds of choice-making situations. Therefore, it has some claim to capturing a piece of "psychological reality." To the best of my knowledge, no similarly broad and plausible psychological theory, based on the idea that people intuit a distinction between doing and allowing, is available to explain Quinn's intuitions. What we have from Quinn is introspective testimony that this is the right explanation, combined with a few anecdotal claims that other people have come to the same opinion. If a reader of Quinn's essay also comes to this opinion, that will be no more than one additional piece of introspective evidence. By the ordinary epistemic standards of decision psychology, the prospect-theoretic explanation is the one we should accept.

As I mentioned earlier, the example I have chosen to discuss is not the only example in the philosophical literature purporting to exhibit an intuitive moral difference between doing and allowing. Someone might argue that unless prospect theory explains all, or at least most, of the intuitions people have when they consider these other examples, it is implausible to claim that it accounts for Quinn's intuitions. I disagree. The requirement that prospect theory account for all of these cases would be question begging. To require of a psychological theory that it explain all of the intuitions in some class of examples described as "cases where people respond to a distinction between doing and allowing" is to assume that we know antecedently that the intuitions in all these cases are due to a distinction between doing and allowing. It may be, in fact, that several different unnoticed psychological mechanisms account for the responses of subjects in these cases and that the distinction between doing and allowing is a superficial characterization without psychological reality.[12]

I have *not* made the claim that prospect theory provides a distinction among Quinn's rescue cases that is morally significant. I do not see why anyone would think the distinction is morally significant, but perhaps there is some argument I have not thought of. If the distinction is not morally significant, then Quinn's thought experiments cannot play the role in his argument that he intends for them to play. It is crucial for Quinn that the intuitions he elicts be moral intuitions, since he wants to argue that our moral intuitions both support the Doctrine of Doing and Allowing and conflict with consequentialism. Further, he wants the doctrine of rights which he develops in his essay to explain these very moral intuitions. But to the extent that the intuitions elicited by Quinn's thought experiments are explained by prospect theory, they are not moral intuitions at all.

To put the same point differently, suppose someone argues that even if the prospect-theoretic account of the differing responses to the Rescue Dilemmas is not morally significant, these differing responses to the Rescue Dilemmas can still play a role in ethical argumentation, if the argumentative method being used is one of reflective equilibrium.[13] The suggestion is that if we appeal to our intuitions about the Rescue Dilemmas in the course of constructing a moral theory by getting our intuitions into reflective equilibrium with our theory, then the fact that our intuitions have their origins in prospect theory won't matter any more than it would matter if our intuitions had their origins in religious training. But when we engage in reflective-equilibrium reasoning we are, to paraphrase Rawls, looking to see if the principles we formulate match our considered ethical convictions. The principles we formulate, then, must be brought into reflective equilibrium with moral judgments (whatever the origin of these). My contention is that when Quinn, or anyone else, judges that there is a difference in what it is permissible to do in the two Rescue Dilemmas, they are mistaken in thinking that they are making a moral judgment at all.

V

Philosophers who have a certain conception of psychological theory, together with a certain conception of the nature of reasoning, might argue that the suggestion I have made completely misses the mark.[14] Quinn is trying to articulate some pattern of reasoning shared by everyone whose intuitions about the Rescue Dilemmas are similar to his own. His suggestion is that there is such a pattern of reasoning, and it involves making a distinction between doing and allowing. I have argued that prospect theory provides us with a different and conflicting account of the pattern of reasoning common to those who share Quinn's intuitions about the Rescue Dilemmas. But my suggestion obviously presupposes that prospect theory should be understood as positing that, in certain circumstances, people engage in processes of reasoning of which they are unaware and, perhaps, processes of reasoning to which they cannot gain conscious access even with careful introspection. The objector I have in mind points to this unconscious aspect of the mechanism posited by prospect theory and concludes that this mechanism should not be regarded as a process of reasoning at all. Rather, we should think of prospect theory as providing us with a causal law of psychological nature, according to which certain factors cause, or incline, a subject to form certain preferences. To the extent that this causal law is expressed in language appropriate to processes of reasoning in the ordinary sense of the term 'reasoning', the language is misleading. And, says this objector, the language appears to have misled me in this article.

Someone might base this objection on either of two related arguments. The first argument goes like this.

In order for a process of thought to be reasoning, it must be subject to norms or standards of correctness. There must be a distinction between correct and incorrect reasoning, between reasoning that is performed as it ought to be and reasoning that is not performed as it ought to be. A philosopher will be inclined to believe this to the extent that she sees the concept of a process of reasoning as closely connected to the concept of having reasons for a belief or an action. If one has a reason for a belief or an action, it will be a more or less good reason or a more or less bad reason. It will be subject to evaluation. A sequence of psychological states occurring in a person should be called a 'process of reasoning' only if it constitutes the person coming to "have a reason." On this conception of the meaning of the expression 'process of reasoning', any sequence of psychological states that deserves to be called a 'process of reasoning' must be subject to evaluation, just as the having of a reason is subject to evaluation. Someone else might deny this close conceptual tie between the concept of a process of reasoning and the concept of having a reason. The philosopher I have in mind accepts the tie.

The argument continues along the following lines. There can be no standards of correctness for reasoning that is in principle hidden from view. If reasoning is hidden from view, how could standards of correctness ever develop, and how could they ever be applied?

The second argument starts with the premise that, according to prospect theory, some aspects of the so-called reasoning it posits are not under the control of the subject. For instance, the language used to formulate a decision problem can result in a subject's choosing one or another neutral outcome to serve as a reference point for the evaluation of other outcomes. It appears that subjects often have little, if any, control over this choice of neutral outcome. But 'ought' implies 'can'. If a subject ought to reason in a certain way, then it must be up to the subject to voluntarily choose to reason in that way. So the concepts of what the subject ought and ought not to do cannot be applied coherently to these thought processes. Therefore, they are not processes subject to norms or standards of correctness and thus are not processes one should call 'reasoning'.

This second argument clearly is off the mark as it stands. Some very simple instances of logically valid argument are so compelling that it may be impossible for most people to accept the premises while rejecting the conclusion. Probably an argument in the form of "A, B, therefore, A and B" would compel the acceptance of most adults. So it will not do to claim that genuine reasoning always is under the control of an agent to accept or reject.

But the second argument nevertheless is getting at a legitimate worry. The thought processes posited by prospect theory are outside the voluntary control of the subject, not because they compel assent, but because they are hidden from view and completely closed to critical appraisal. So the second argument really is a special case of the first. The question, then, is whether we should accept the first argument.

I am granting, for the sake of argument, that a thought process must be subject to standards of correctness in order to qualify as reasoning. Some psychological theories posit unnoticed processes that fail to meet this criterion, even though psychologists sometimes call such processes 'reasoning'. For instance, a theory in the psychology of vision might explain the seeing of illusory contours by positing a gap-filling process that obeys a certain law. The law might be expressible as a differential equation or by some other mathematical relationship. Presumably subjects are not aware that their vision is governed by this law.

When one of these gap-filling processes occurs in a person, the process itself does not constitute the person's "having a reason" for believing contours exist where, in fact, there are no physical contours. As a result of the gap-filling process, it may "look to the person as though there are contours." This fact would be a reason for the person to believe there really are contours. But it is plausible to think that this fact is a result of the gap-filling process and is not strictly identical to it. Even if the gap-filling process is strictly identical to the fact of "it looking as though there are contours," we should not conclude that the gap-filling process constitutes a reason, since the seemingly relational predicate 'is a reason for' is nonextensional at both ends.[15]

No standards of correctness apply to these posited gap-filling processes. So, on the assumption I am making for purposes of argument, these processes are not instances of 'reasoning'.

The question is whether every psychological theory positing unnoticed "thought" processes shares this feature. The answer, clearly, is no; and prospect theory is a good example with which to illustrate the difference. Prospect theory posits various thought processes that are unnoticed by the subject in whom they occur. Therefore, those very thought processes are not open to criticism in ordinary circumstances. But many of these thought processes are processes of a kind that can occur in people consciously and voluntarily. And when they do, they are instances of 'reasoning' in any ordinary sense of the term, subject to standards of correctness, and readily criticizable by the subject and by others who become aware of them. The unnoticed thought processes posited by prospect theory are subject to standards of correctness, because other thought processes of the same form are routinely subjected to standards of correctness. An instance of reasoning is subject to a standard of correctness if it is an instance of a form that is thus criticizable. This is an old idea, and a very good one.

For example, suppose a board of directors is dutifully making its annual performance evaluation of the chief executive officer (CEO). Some members of the board claim that the CEO had a poor year, since the company suffered a net loss for the year. Other members of the board disagree. They argue that the CEO had a good year, since the beginning-of-the-year projections were that every company in the industry would suffer much greater losses than this company eventually suffered, and all the other companies did, in fact, suffer much greater losses. The CEO did a better job of weathering the general downturn than any of her competitors. In order to finally decide how to evaluate the CEO, members of the board must decide which reference point to use. Should they choose the point where there are no gains or losses for the year, or should they choose a point defined by the projected losses for companies in the industry as a whole? The issue of which reference point to choose is likely to be matter of debate. Standards of correctness and incorrectness could be brought to bear on the choice of a reference point, and such standards eventually would have to be brought to bear.

The formal analogy between what the board of directors must do and what, according to prospect theory, individual decision-makers often do is obvious. Of course, prospect theory posits many other kinds of thought processes in addition to choosing reference points, but, for many of these other processes, there are equally familiar analogs engaged in by people consciously, publicly, and in a way that is subject to standards of correctness.

I conclude that the objections I have raised to my earlier suggestion both fail. It is therefore possible that prospect theory, augmented by the empirical hypotheses I described earlier, provides the correct account of the reasoning engaged in by people who come to have Quinn's intuitions concerning his Rescue Dilemmas. If this is so, then Quinn's philosophical thought experiments do not provide us with an argument for his philosophical conclusions. What this shows, I believe, is that the extraction of philosophical conclusions from philosophical thought experiments is at least sometimes an a posteriori, not an a priori, matter. The question naturally arises whether it ever is an a priori matter. I suspect the answer is no.

Should we conclude that the important philosophical method of thought experimentation is valueless if it is not a priori? I think the jury is still out. It may be that philosophers are capable of making fairly accurate judgments concerning their processes of reasoning most of the time. Quinn's thought experiments may be an unusually unfavorable case. Or it may be that misjudgments are the rule. For example, philosophers with a developed set of philosophical views may be just as susceptible to experimenter effects as are linguists who have developed views.[16] The matter must be empirically studied.[17]

Notes

I am indebted to Joseph Camp, Robyn Dawes, Joel Pust, Alexander Rosenberg, Eldar Shafir, Michael Thompson, Mark Wilson, two editors of *Ethics*, and audiences at the University of Pittsburgh, Carnegie Mellon University, and the "Rethinking Intuition" conference held at the University of Notre Dame in April 1996 for their helpful criticisms and suggestions.

1. Warren Quinn, "Actions, Intentions, and Consequences: The Doctrine of Doing and Allowing," in *Morality and Action* (Cambridge: Cambridge University Press, 1993), 149.

2. The Doctrine of Doing and Allowing and this thought experiment are originally the work of Professor P. Foote. See P. Foote, "Killing and Letting Die," in *Abortion: Moral and Legal Perspectives*, ed. Jay Garfield (Amherst: University of Massachusetts Press, 1984), 178–185.

3. Quinn, *Morality and Action*, 152.

4. Quinn, *Morality and Action*, 167.

5. For an account of prospect theory, see D. Kahneman and A. Tversky, "Prospect Theory: An Analysis of Decision under Risk," *Econometrica* 47 (1979): 263–91. By "classical expected utility theory" I mean to refer to the theories found in J. Von Neumann and O. Morgenstern, *Theory of Games and Economic Behavior* (Princeton, N.J.: Princeton University Press, 1972); and in L. Savage, *The Foundations of Statistics*, 2nd rev. ed. (New York: Dover, 1972).

6. Problem 2 is obtained from problem 1 by increasing the original amount by $200 and subtracting this amount from both options.

7. An expected utility maximizer would not exhibit this pattern, since any person who is maximizing expected utility would choose the first option in each problem or the second option in each problem.

8. The other operations include combining probabilities associated with identical outcomes, segregating risky from riskless components of prospects, discarding

components that are shared by all of the available prospects, rounding off probabilities or outcomes, and rejecting dominated alternatives. For a full discussion of these processes, see Kahneman and Tversky, "Prospect Theory," 274.

9. Positive and negative prospects are evaluated in the following way. In the editing phase, they are segregated into two components, a riskless component, which is the minimum loss or gain certain to be received, and a risky component, comprised of the additional gain or loss at stake. These prospects are then evaluated in the following way: if $p + q = 1$ and either $x > y > 0$ or $x < y < 0$, then $D(x, p; y, q) = v(y) + w(p) [v(x) - v(y)]$. This value equals the value of the riskless component, plus the difference between the two outcomes multiplied by the weight associated with the outcome with the greater absolute value. See Kahneman and Tversky, "Prospect Theory" 276.

10. Kahneman and Tversky, "Prospect Theory" 279.

11. Notice that no such hypothesis is needed for the analysis of the experiments reported by Kahneman and Tversky. They are concerned to explain the order in which subjects prefer certain possible actions in different decision problems. To do this, they must hypothesize that, in each decision problem, a subject arrives at a D value for various alternative actions, but they are never required to hypothesize that these D values can be compared from one decision problem to the other.

12. Nevertheless, I suspect prospect theory does explain most of these intuitions, although I will not try to survey them here.

13. This is a version of an objection offered by one of the editors of *Ethics*.

14. I am especially indebted to Joseph Camp for many helpful discussions of the issues treated in this section.

15. Assume that I am at a gym and that I am wearing my glasses. A thief to my left steals my pocketbook off a chair. Fortunately, there is a police officer in uniform to my right. Then, (a) *the thief to my left stealing my pocketbook* is a reason for (b) *my calling to the police officer to my right.* If my glasses are off, I will not be so lucky because (c) *the dark figure to my left holding a dark object* is not a reason for (d) *my calling to the dark figure to my right.* One can argue that (a) and (c) are strictly identical states and that (b) and (d) are strictly identical states. 'Is a reason for' resembles 'implies' in its logic.

16. See W. Labov, "Empirical Foundations of Linguistic Theory," in *The Scope of American Linguistics*, ed. R. Austerlitz (Ghent: Peter De Ridder, 1975), 77–133; and N. Spencer, "Differences between Linguists and Nonlinguists in Intuitions of Grammaticality-Acceptability," *Journal of Psycholinguistic Research* 2 (1973): 83–98 (cited in Labov).

17. It was called to my attention after this article was written that Robert Nozick points to the "strong similarity" between the doing and allowing distinction and framing effects in *The Nature of Rationality* (Princeton, N.J.: Princeton University Press, 1995), 60.

INDEX